First World War
and Army of Occupation
War Diary
France, Belgium and Germany

25 DIVISION
7 Infantry Brigade
Worcestershire Regiment
3rd Battalion
1 January 1916 - 31 October 1917

WO95/2244/1

The Naval & Military Press Ltd
www.nmarchive.com
Published in association with The National Archives

Published by

The Naval & Military Press Ltd

Unit 10 Ridgewood Industrial Park,

Uckfield, East Sussex,

TN22 5QE England

Tel: +44 (0) 1825 749494

www.naval-military-press.com

www.nmarchive.com

This diary has been reprinted in facsimile from the original. Any imperfections are inevitably reproduced and the quality may fall short of modern type and cartographic standards.

© **Crown Copyright**
Images reproduced by permission of The National Archives, London, England, 2015.

Contents

Document type	Place/Title	Date From	Date To
Heading	This item has been conserved as part of the WO95 Digitisation Project Please keep this sheet at the front of the box		
Heading	WO95/2244-1		
Heading	3rd Bn Worcs Regt Nov 1915-Oct 1917 From 3 Div 7 Bde To 74 Bde Same Div.		
Heading	3rd Divisions 3/Worc Regt Nov Vol XV Nov 15 & Oct 17		
War Diary		01/11/1917	04/12/1917
Heading	25th Div 3/Worcester Regt Dec Vol XVI		
War Diary		05/12/1917	31/12/1917
Heading	3rd Battalion. Worcestershire Regiment. January 1916		
Heading	7th Bde 25th Div 3rd Worcester Regt Jan Vol XVII		
War Diary		01/01/1916	31/01/1916
Heading	3rd Battalion. Worcestershire Regiment February 1916		
War Diary		01/02/1916	29/02/1916
Heading	3rd Battalion Worcestershire Regiment March 1916		
War Diary		01/03/1916	31/03/1916
Heading	3rd Battalion Worcestershire Regiment April 1916		
War Diary	Active Service	01/04/1916	30/04/1916
Heading	3rd Battalion Worcestershire Regiment May 1916		
War Diary	Active Service	01/05/1916	31/05/1916
Heading	3rd Battalion. Worcestershire Regiment June 1916		
War Diary	Active Service	01/06/1916	30/06/1916
Heading	3rd Battalion Worcestershire Regiment. July 1916		
War Diary		01/07/1916	29/07/1916
Miscellaneous	Reserve Army Special Order	16/07/1916	16/07/1916
Miscellaneous	Special Divisional Order	17/07/1916	17/07/1916
Miscellaneous	Special Divisional Order	08/07/1916	08/07/1916
Miscellaneous	74th Infantry Brigade		
Miscellaneous	A Form. Messages And Signals.	17/07/1916	17/07/1916
Miscellaneous	3rd Bn Worcestershire Regt. Casualties for July 1916		
Heading	3rd Battalion Worcestershire Regiment August 1916		
War Diary	Active Serv	01/08/1916	14/08/1916
War Diary	A S	15/08/1918	29/08/1918
Miscellaneous	25th Divn. G. 472	25/08/1916	25/08/1916
Miscellaneous	Report On Operation 3rd Worcestershire	27/08/1916	27/08/1916
Miscellaneous	Casualties from 1st August to 26th August 1916		
Heading	3rd Worcester Regt. September 1916		
War Diary	Active Service	30/08/1916	29/09/1916
Heading	3rd Battalion. Worcestershire Regiment. October 1916		
War Diary	Active Service	30/09/1916	31/10/1916
Miscellaneous	3rd Bn Worcestershire Regt		
Miscellaneous	Casualties October 1916		
Heading	3rd Battalion Worcestershire Regiment November 1916		
War Diary	Active Service	01/11/1916	30/11/1916
Miscellaneous	Casualties November 1916		
Heading	3rd Battalion Worcestershire Regiment. December 1916		
War Diary	Active Service	01/12/1916	31/12/1916
Miscellaneous	3rd Bn Worcestershire Regt		

Type	Description	Start	End
War Diary	Active Service	01/01/1917	31/01/1917
Miscellaneous	Casualties during the month of January 1917		
War Diary		01/02/1917	31/03/1917
Miscellaneous	Casualties during March 1917	31/03/1917	31/03/1917
War Diary	La Creche Area	01/04/1917	04/04/1917
War Diary	St Marie Cappel	05/04/1917	12/04/1917
War Diary	Outtersteene	13/04/1917	13/04/1917
War Diary	Le Bizet	14/04/1917	16/04/1917
War Diary	Trenches	17/04/1917	20/04/1917
War Diary	Outtersteene	21/04/1917	29/04/1917
War Diary	Strazeele	30/04/1917	30/04/1917
Miscellaneous	3rd Bn Worcestershire Regt	01/05/1917	01/05/1917
War Diary	Strazeele Area	01/05/1917	04/05/1917
War Diary	Ebblinghem	04/04/1917	04/04/1917
War Diary	Etrehem	05/05/1917	18/05/1917
War Diary	Strazeele	19/05/1917	19/05/1917
War Diary	Bailleul Area	20/05/1917	23/05/1917
War Diary	Neuve Eglise	24/05/1917	31/05/1917
Miscellaneous	Casualties for Month of May 1917		
War Diary	Neuve Eglise T.1.d 2.8	01/06/1917	02/06/1917
War Diary	Trenches N 36.d.1.5	02/06/1917	02/06/1917
War Diary	Ravelsburg S17.C.1.8	03/06/1917	06/06/1917
War Diary	Trenches Onslow Trench N 36 d.2.3	06/06/1917	06/06/1917
War Diary	Trenches N 36.d.2.3	07/06/1917	07/06/1917
War Diary	Messines Ridge	07/06/1917	09/06/1917
War Diary	Middle Farm	10/06/1917	11/06/1917
War Diary	Bivouacs T 10.C.1.9	12/06/1917	13/06/1917
War Diary	Neuve Eglise	13/06/1917	13/06/1917
War Diary	Messines Ridge	14/06/1917	22/06/1917
War Diary	Ravelsberg 17.C.1.8	23/06/1917	23/06/1917
War Diary	Swartenbrouck	24/06/1917	24/06/1917
War Diary	St Venant	25/06/1917	25/06/1917
War Diary	Westrehem	26/06/1917	26/06/1917
War Diary	Coyecque	27/06/1917	30/06/1917
Miscellaneous	Casualties During Month Of June		
Operation(al) Order(s)	Appendix A 3rd Bn The Worcestershire Regt. O.O. No 142	01/06/1917	01/06/1917
Miscellaneous	Appendix F		
War Diary	Coyecque	01/07/1917	07/07/1917
War Diary	Ypres	08/07/1917	08/07/1917
War Diary	Hooge Trenches	09/07/1917	10/07/1917
War Diary	Ypres	15/07/1917	23/07/1917
War Diary	Hooge Clarf	24/07/1917	29/07/1917
Miscellaneous	Casualties for July 1917 Appendix "A"		
Operation(al) Order(s)	3rd Bn The Worcestershire Regt. O.O. 152 App B	30/07/1917	30/07/1917
War Diary		01/08/1917	30/08/1917
Miscellaneous	Casualties during Month Of August 1917		
War Diary		31/08/1917	30/09/1917
Miscellaneous	Casualties During September 1917		
War Diary	Burbure	01/10/1917	03/10/1917
War Diary	Bethune	04/10/1917	04/10/1917
War Diary	Givenchy Festubert Sector	05/10/1917	11/10/1917
War Diary	Windy Corner	12/10/1917	17/10/1917
War Diary	Givenchy Festubert Sector	17/10/1917	23/10/1917
War Diary	Gorre Chateau	23/10/1917	29/10/1917
War Diary	Givenchy Festubert Sector	29/10/1917	31/10/1917

Miscellaneous	Casualties During October
Miscellaneous	7th Inf Bde

This item has been conserved as part of the WO95 Digitisation Project

Please keep this sheet at the front of the box

No 96/2244/1

25TH DIVISION
7TH INFY BDE

3RD BN WORCS REGT
NOV 1915-OCT 1917

from 3 Div 7 Bde

To 74 Bde SAME DIV.

Army Form C. 2118.

WAR DIARY
or
INTELLIGENCE SUMMARY. 3/Worcestershire Regt.
(Erase heading not required.)

November 1915

Instructions regarding War Diaries and Intelligence Summaries are contained in F. S. Regs., Part II. and the Staff Manual respectively. Title pages will be prepared in manuscript.

Place	Date	Hour	Summary of Events and Information	Remarks and references to Appendices
	1st November		Relieved by 10th Bn Cheshire Regt — Went into Billets at Papot near Niepple as Divisional Reserve.	
	2nd "		Ditto	
	3rd "		Ditto	

[signature]

1875 W¹. W.593/826 1,000,000 4/15 J.B.C. & A. A.D.S.S./Forms/C. 2118.

WAR DIARY
or
INTELLIGENCE SUMMARY

(Erase heading not required.)

Army Form C. 2118

Place	Date	Hour	Summary of Events and Information	Remarks and references to Appendices
	4th November		In Billets at Papot near Nieppe, as Divisional Reserve.	
	5th	"		

McVeagh Major

Army Form C. 2118

WAR DIARY
or
INTELLIGENCE SUMMARY
(Erase heading not required.)

Place	Date	Hour	Summary of Events and Information	Remarks and references to Appendices
	5th Nov.		In billets at Pabot near Niepps in Divinal Reserve.	
	6th Nov.		ditto	
	7th	"	Relieved 10th Cheshires in left Sector of Ploegsteert Wood relief completed by 12 noon. 8th Loyal North Lancs holding right sector of 7th Brigade line — Canadian Division on our left.	
	8th	"	ditto	
	9th	"	ditto	
	10th	"	ditto	
	11	"	ditto	
	12th	"	ditto	"
	13th	"	Relieved by 10th Cheshires — Relief completed by 12 noon — went into Brigade Reserve at PIGGARIES.	R & F Killed, wounded 1.

Ph. Whyhyh. Major

Army Form C. 2118

WAR DIARY
or
INTELLIGENCE SUMMARY
(Erase heading not required.)

Instructions regarding War Diaries and Intelligence Summaries are contained in F. S. Regs., Part II. and the Staff Manual respectively. Title Pages will be prepared in manuscript.

Place	Date	Hour	Summary of Events and Information	Remarks and references to Appendices
	14th Nov		In Brigade Reserve at Piggaries.	R of 1 Wounded
	15th "		ditto "	
	16th "		ditto "	R of 2 Wounded
	17th "		ditto "	
	18th "		ditto "	
	19th "		Relieved 10th Cheshire Regt in left Sector of Ploegsteert Wood relief completed by 12 Noon. 8 Loyal North Lancs holding right Sector. Canadian Division on our left.	
	20th "		In Trenches.	
	21st "		do "	
	22nd "		do "	
	23rd "		do "	

Ed. John Lyde L. Major

Army Form C. 2118

WAR DIARY
or
INTELLIGENCE SUMMARY
(Erase heading not required.)

Instructions regarding War Diaries and Intelligence Summaries are contained in F. S. Regs., Part II. and the Staff Manual respectively. Title Pages will be prepared in manuscript.

Place	Date	Hour	Summary of Events and Information	Remarks and references to Appendices
24th	Nov.		Relieved by 10th Cheshire Regt - 2chief (coy) left 1pm moved into Divisional Reserve at Papot near Nieppe. In billets at Papot	
	25th		ditto	
	26th		ditto	
	27th		ditto	
	28th		ditto	
	29th		Relieved 10th Cheshires in Trenches Ploegsteert Wood	
	30th		In Trenches	
	1st Dec		ditto "	R + 1 Wounded
	2nd "		ditto "	R + 1 Wounded
	3 "		ditto "	
	4th "		Relieved by 10th Cheshire Regt - moved into Brigade Reserve at Nigga Ries	

(signed) J Hughes Major

T.15

3/ Commissioner Raj
Das
vol. XVI

12/7934

Army Form C. 2118

WAR DIARY
or
INTELLIGENCE SUMMARY
(Erase heading not required.)

Instructions regarding War Diaries and Intelligence Summaries are contained in F. S. Regs., Part II. and the Staff Manual respectively. Title Pages will be prepared in manuscript.

Place	Date	Hour	Summary of Events and Information	Remarks and references to Appendices
December	5th		In Brigade Reserve at PIGGERIES.	
	6th		d ito	
	7th		do	
	8th		do	
	9th		Relieved 10th Cheshire Regt in trenches PLOEGSTEERT Wood	1 R & F killed
	10th		In trenches	
	11th		In trenches	1 R & F killed
	12th		In trenches	3 R & F wounded
	13th		In trenches	1 R & F killed
	14th		Relieved by 10th Cheshire Regt went into Divisional Reserve at PAPOT	
	15th		At PAPOT	
	16th			
	17th			
	18th			

Army Form C. 2118

WAR DIARY
or
INTELLIGENCE SUMMARY
(Erase heading not required.)

Instructions regarding War Diaries and Intelligence Summaries are contained in F. S. Regs, Part II. and the Staff Manual respectively. Title Pages will be prepared in manuscript.

Place	Date	Hour	Summary of Events and Information	Remarks and references to Appendices
December	19th		Relieved 10th Cheshire Regiment in trenches PLOEGSTEERT WOOD.	
	20th		In trenches	R o F 2 WOUNDED
	21st		do	
	22nd		do	
	23rd		do	R & F 1 WOUNDED
	24th		Relieved by 10th Cheshire Regiment in trenches & went into Brigade Reserve at PIGGERRIES	
	25th		(Christmas Day) at PIGGERRIES	
	26th		do	
	27th		do	R o F 1 WOUNDED
	28th		do	
	29th		Relieved 10th Cheshire Regiment in trenches PLOEGSTEERTWOOD	
	30th		In trenches	R o F 1 KILLED
	31st		do	

A. Moores Fox Capt.
Actg/Lt - 3rd Worc. Reg.

1875 Wt. W593/826 1,000,000 4/15 J.B.C. & A. A.D.S.S./Forms/C. 2118.

7th INFANTRY BDE.

25th DIVISION.

3rd BATTALION.

WORCESTERSHIRE REGIMENT.

JANUARY 1916

3

3rd Warwickshire Regt

1 am / Vol XVII

7th Bde 25th Div.

T.16

WAR DIARY
or
INTELLIGENCE SUMMARY

(Erase heading not required.)

Army Form C. 2118

Instructions regarding War Diaries and Intelligence Summaries are contained in F.S. Regs., Part II and the Staff Manual respectively. Title Pages will be prepared in manuscript.

Place	Date	Hour	Summary of Events and Information	Remarks and references to Appendices
January	1		In in trenches in PLOEGSTEERT WOOD	
"	2		do	R.O.F. 1 KILLED 3 WOUNDED
"	3		Relieved by 10th Cheshire Regiment from trenches & went into Divisional reserve at PAPOT	R.O.F. 1 WOUNDED
"	4		At PAPOT	
"	5		do	
"	6		do	R.O.F. 1 WOUNDED
"	7		Relieved 10th Cheshire Regiment in trenches at PLOEGSTEERT WOOD	R.O.F. 1 KILLED
"	8		In trenches do	
"	9		do	R.O.F. 1 KILLED 1 WOUNDED
"	10		do	
"	11		do	R.O.F. 1 WOUNDED
"	12		do	R.O.F. 1 KILLED 3 WOUNDED
"	13		Relieved by 10th Cheshire Regiment from trenches & went into Brigade reserve at PIGGERIES	
"	14		At PIGGERIES	

E Durnley Lt Col
3rd Worc Regt

WAR DIARY
or
INTELLIGENCE SUMMARY

(Erase heading not required.)

Army Form C. 2118

Place	Date	Hour	Summary of Events and Information	Remarks and references to Appendices
January	15		Bn in Brigade Reserve at PIGGERIES	1 KILLED R of F
"	16		do	
"	17		do	
"	18		do	
"	19		Relieved 10th Cheshire Regiment from trenches in PLOEGSTEERT WOOD	R of F 1 WOUNDED
"	20		In trenches	
"	21		do	
"	22		do	R of F 2 KILLED 6 WOUNDED
"	23		do	
"	24		Relieved by 5th Cameron Highlanders from trenches & went into Brigade reserve at PAPOT	
"	25		Moved to LA CRECHE area for the night	
"	26		Moved to Corps reserve in OUTTERSTEEN area	
"	27		do " " "	
"	28		do " " "	
"	29		do	
"	30		do	
"	31		do	

7th INAFNRY BDE.

25th DIVISION.

3rd BATTALION.

WORCESTERSHIRE REGIMENT

FEBRUARY 1916

Army Form C. 2118

3/29ᵃ
FEB. 1916

WAR DIARY
or
INTELLIGENCE SUMMARY
(Erase heading not required.)

Instructions regarding War Diaries and Intelligence Summaries are contained in F. S. Regs., Part II. and the Staff Manual respectively. Title Pages will be prepared in manuscript.

J.17.

Place	Date	Hour	Summary of Events and Information	Remarks and references to Appendices
February	1		In 2nd Corps reserve in OUTTERSTEEN area	
	2		do --- Company training	
	3		do --- do	
	4		do --- do	
	5		do --- do	
	6		do --- Church Parade	
	7		do --- Company training	
	8		do --- do	
	9		do --- Inspected by G.O.C 2ⁿᵈ ARMY on Brigade Route March.	
	10		do --- Company training	
	11		do --- do	
	12		do --- do	
	13		do --- Church Parade	
	14		do --- Company training	

E. Standly

Army Form C. 2118

WAR DIARY
INTELLIGENCE SUMMARY
(Erase heading not required.)

Instructions regarding War Diaries and Intelligence Summaries are contained in F.S. Regs., Part II. and the Staff Manual respectively. Title Pages will be prepared in manuscript.

Place	Date	Hour	Summary of Events and Information	Remarks and references to Appendices
February	15th		In 2nd Corps area in OUTTERSTEEN area. Company training	
"	16th		do — Company training	
"	17th		do — do	
"	18th		do — do	
"	19th		do — Batln. Route March.	
"	20th		do — Church Parade	
"	21st		do — Company training	
"	22nd		do — Brigade training	
"	23rd		do — do	
"	24th		do — Batln. Route March	
"	25th		do — Company training	
"	26th		do — do	
"	27th		do — Church Parade	
"	28th		do — Company training	S. Gurr &c
"	29th		do — do	

7th INFANTRY BDE.

25th DIVISION

3rd BATTALION.

WORCESTERSHIRE REGIMENT

MARCH 1916

Army Form C. 2118

WAR DIARY
or
INTELLIGENCE SUMMARY
(Erase heading not required.)

Instructions regarding War Diaries and Intelligence Summaries are contained in F. S. Regs., Part II. and the Staff Manual respectively. Title Pages will be prepared in manuscript.

Place	Date	Hour	Summary of Events and Information	Remarks and references to Appendices
March	1st		Battalion in 2nd Corps Reserve at OUTTERSTEENE. Company Training.	
"	2nd		" " " " " " Battalion Route March.	
"	3rd		" " " " " " Company Training.	
"	4th		" " " " " " " "	
"	5th		" " " " " " Church Parade.	
"	6th		" " " " " " Brigade Route March.	
"	7th		" " " " " " Company Training.	
"	8th		" " " " " " Battalion Route March.	
"	9th		" " " " " " Company Training.	
"	10th		Battalion commenced move into 17th Corps area. Billeted at ROBECQ for night 10.3.15.	
"	11th		" " resumed " " Billeted at CONTEVILLE.	
"	12th		At CONTEVILLE.	
"	13th		" "	
"	14th		" "	

E. Davidge .... LIEUT. COL.
COMMANDING 3rd WORCESTERSHIRE REGT.

1875 Wt. W593/826 1,000,000 4/15 J.B.C. & A. A.D.S.S./Forms/C. 2118.

Army Form C. 2118

WAR DIARY
or
INTELLIGENCE SUMMARY
(Erase heading not required.)

J. 17ª

Place	Date	Hour	Summary of Events and Information	Remarks and references to Appendices
March	15th		Battalion resumed move into 17th Corps area and marched to PENIN	
"	16th		" in 17th Corps Reserve at PENIN	
"	17th		do	
"	18th		do	Battalion training
"	19th		do	Company training
"	20th		do	Battalion do
"	21st		do	Company Church Parade
"	22nd		do	Battalion Route March
"	23rd		do	Battalion training
"	24th		do	" "
"	25th		do	Battalion Route March
"	26th		do	Battalion training
"	27th		do	Company Church Parade
"	28th		do	Battalion Route March
"	29th		do	Company training
"	30th		do	Battalion Sports
"	31st		do	Company training
				Battalion inspected by Commander in Chief on a Route March

S. Davidge .... LIEUT. COL.
COMMANDING 3rd WORCESTERSHIRE REGT.

7th INFANTRY BDE

25th DIVISION.

3rd BATTALION.

WORCESTERSHIRE REGIMENT

APRIL 1916

WAR DIARY
or
INTELLIGENCE SUMMARY
(Erase heading not required.)

Army Form C. 2118

Instructions regarding War Diaries and Intelligence Summaries are contained in F. S. Regs., Part II. and the Staff Manual respectively. Title Pages will be prepared in manuscript.

Place	Date	Hour	Summary of Events and Information	Remarks and references to Appendices
Aubier Sones	APRIL			CASUALTIES
	2nd		Battalion in 17th Corps Reserve at PENIN. 1 Company Training	
			2 Church Parade	
	3rd		" " " Company Training	
	4th		" " " 3 Battalion Training	
	5th		" " " 4 Brigade Route March	
	6th		" " " 5 Company Training	
	7th		" " " 6 Battalion Route March	
	8th		" " " 7 Company Training	
	9th		" " " 8 Church Parade	
	10th		Battalion moved by Motor lorry to MAROEUIL to relieve 13th Cheshire Regt. of moving fatigues. Two Companies at MAROEUIL and two at ANZIN-ST-AUBIN and ROCLIN COURT	
	11th		Moving fatigues on front line trenches North of ARRAS.	WOUNDED 1 Other Rank
	12th		" " " " " "	
	13th		" " " " " "	
	14th		" " " " " "	

S. Stanly .... LIEUT. COL.
COMMANDING 3rd WORCESTERSHIRE REGT.

WAR DIARY or INTELLIGENCE SUMMARY

Army Form C. 2118

(Erase heading not required.)

Instructions regarding War Diaries and Intelligence Summaries are contained in F. S. Regs., Part II. and the Staff Manual respectively. Title Pages will be prepared in manuscript.

Place	Date	Hour	Summary of Events and Information	Remarks and references to Appendices
ACTIVE SERVICE	APRIL 15th		Working fatigues in front line trenches North of ARRAS.	
	16th		" " " " "	WOUNDED 1 Oth. Rank
	17th		" " " " "	
	18th		" " " " "	
	19th		23rd Division relieved 46th Division from trenches North East of MONT ST ELOY.	
	20th		Battalion in Divisional Reserve at ACQ.	
	20th		" " " " "	
	21st		" " " " "	
	22nd		" " " " "	
	23rd		" " " " "	
	24th		" " " " "	
	25th		" " " " "	
	26th		Battalion relieved 10th Cheshire Regiment from trenches North East of MONT ST ELOY	WOUNDED 2 Oth. Ranks
	27th		In trenches. Enemy's Artillery active on communication trenches during day & night.	{ 1 Officer 3 Oth. Rank Killed 1 Officer 8 Oth. Rank }
	28th		Enemy exploded mine under left Company's (D Coy) outpost line, they entered the Mine but were driven out. The mine exploded about 7.15 P.M.	6.0— Missing beheld Friend killed 47 Wounded

Spain
LIEUT COL
COMMANDING 3rd WORCESTERSHIRE REGT.

WAR DIARY
or
INTELLIGENCE SUMMARY

(Erase heading not required.)

Army Form C. 2118

Place	Date	Hour	Summary of Events and Information	Remarks and references to Appendices
RITIVE SECTOR S9	April 29th		Two platoons of A Company, supported by two platoons of B Coy, were ordered to gain and consolidate near top of crater of mine exploded on the 28th inst. The assault was made at 8.15 P.M after obstinate preparation, but owing to very heavy Machine Gun and rifle fire from gap, no headway was made. A second attempt was made at 1.45 A.M with the same result.	KILLED 1 Officer 7 Other Ranks MISSING 6 to 10 2 Other Ranks WOUNDED 1 Officer 42 Other Ranks
	30th		In accordance with instructions from F.O.O 7th Inf Bde that it was essential to gain and consolidate the near lip of crater, in front of left centre company's outpost line, an assault was made by a party of 30 other ranks and one officer of C Company, supported by 2 Lewis Guns. The enemy retired and the near lip was gained and consolidated.	WOUNDED 6 Other Ranks KILLED 1 Other Rank

Sd. [signature]

LT. COL.
COMMANDING 3rd WORCESTERSHIRE REGT.

7th INFANTRY BDE,

25th DIVISION.

3rd BATTALION.

WORCESTERSHIRE REGIMENT

MAY 1916

WAR DIARY or INTELLIGENCE SUMMARY

Army Form C. 2118

3 Worcesters Regt

Place	Date	Hour	Summary of Events and Information	Remarks and references to Appendices
ACTIVE SERVICE	MAY			CASUALTIES
	1		Bn relieved from trenches North East of MONT ST. ELOY by 10th Cheshire Regt & proceeded to Bd. Reserve on dug-outs on BETHUNE ROAD. Batn Hq at MONT ST ELOY. Working parties furnished for front line trenches.	Other ranks 2 K, 1 W
	2		Battn in Bd. Reserve. Working parties furnished for front line trenches.	
	3		" " " " "	
	4		" " " " "	
	5		" " " " "	
	6		" " " " "	
	7		" " " " "	
	8		" " " " "	
	9		Bn relieve 10th Cheshire Regt from trenches North East of MONT ST ELOY	Other ranks 3 W
	10		Enemy shelled most of the day, fire chiefly directed on communication trenches.	4 W
	11		Quiet day. Enemy active during night.	
	12		Quiet day and night	Officers 2 W Other ranks 2 K 2 W
	13		In accordance with instructions from ? of Inf Bde H.Q. an attempt was made to rush enemy post on gate to the left of BROADMARSH Salby by an officer and four other ranks, but the post was much stronger than was	7 W

1875 Wt. W 593/826 1,000,000 4/15 J.B.C. & A. A.D.S.S./Forms/C.2118.

.... LIEUT. COL.
COMMANDING 3rd WORCESTERSHIRE REGT.

WAR DIARY
or
INTELLIGENCE SUMMARY
(Erase heading not required.)

Army Form C. 2118

Place	Date MAY	Hour	Summary of Events and Information	Remarks and references to Appendices
ACTIVE SERVICE	13th		anticipated, after throwing bombs and firing into crater, the party returned.	Officers 1K { Other ranks 2K, 3W.
	14th		Quiet day and night.	Other ranks 1W.
	15th		Enemy shelled communication trenches during the day. Quiet night.	Other ranks 1W.
	16th		Quiet day and night.	
	17th		Bn relieved from trenches by 10th Cheshire Regt & proceeded to Dumbarton Other ranks 3K, 7W, 1M. huts & bivouacs at MONT ST ELOY. Under orders to move at 2 an hours notice.	
	18th		Bn in Divisional Reserve at MONT ST ELOY. Standing by.	
	19th		" "	
	20th		" "	
	21st		Enemy put gas shells into MONT ST ELOY starting at 5 P.M. Enemy attacked G SECTOR and portion of P, after very heavy bombardment. Battn moved up to BETHUNE road	
	22nd		Battn relieved 10th Cheshire Regt from trenches which were frantically demolished.	Officers 1W. { Other ranks 7K, 24W, 1M.
	23rd		Enemy shelled most of the day, particular attention being paid to communication trenches. Orders received from Brigade to retake the portion of P. Officers 1K, 1W. Artillery preparation of P. hitherto captured by enemy by the 2/1st Attack commenced at 8.25 P.M. The Other ranks 5K, 63W, 1M.

S. Dandy .... LIEUT COL.
COMMANDING 3rd WORCESTERSHIRE REGT.

Army Form C. 2118

WAR DIARY
or
INTELLIGENCE SUMMARY
(Erase heading not required.)

Instructions regarding War Diaries and Intelligence Summaries are contained in F.S. Regs., Part II. and the Staff Manual respectively. Title Pages will be prepared in manuscript.

Place	Date	Hour	Summary of Events and Information	Remarks and references to Appendices
ACTIVE SERVICE	23rd		Wind was again but owing to the Brigade on our left being unable to advance and very heavy rifle attack was opened from the left and had to fall back to firing attack was opened from the right and eventually a line was established about 30 yards to the left.	Offrs. wnds. 2 K. 3 W.
	24th		Enemy very active with Minnenwerfer, otherwise quiet	
	25th		Quiet day and night	
	26th		Enemy shelled communication trenches. Wire reported taken down by enemy in front of A Company. Necessary precautions taken. Enemy blew up small mine about 8.10 PM in front of A Company, near it was occupied and consolidated.	Officers 1 K Offrs. mds. 9 W.
	27th		Quiet day and night	Officers 1 K Other ranks 2 K
	28th		Enemy's artillery active on trenches	Officers 1 K Othr. ranks 1 K 3 W
	29th		Quiet day. Bombing activity during night.	Other ranks 3 W.
	30th		Quiet day. Bombing activity during night in our trenches	
	31st		Quiet day and night.	

Grainger .... LIEUT. COL.

COMMANDING 3rd WORCESTERSHIRE REGT.

7th INFANTRY BDE

25th DIVISION.

3rd BATTALION,

WORCESTERSHIRE REGIMENT

JUNE 1916

WAR DIARY or INTELLIGENCE SUMMARY

3 Worcester

Army Form C. 2118

1916

Place	Date	Hour	Summary of Events and Information	Remarks and references to Appendices
ACTIVE SERVICE	JUNE 1		Battalion relieved from trenches by 1/4 Seaforth Highlanders. Heavily shelled all day & night. Relief delayed accordingly. On relief Battalion proceeded to ECOIVRES.	CASUALTIES Officers 2 W OR 7 K 9 W 1 M
	2		In billets at ECOIVRES. Battalion marched to AVERDOIGT starting at 8 P.M.	
	3		In billets at AVERDOIGT. Company training	
	4		" " " "	
	5		" " " "	
	6		" " " Attack	
	7		" " " "	
	8		" " " Battalion "	
	9		" " " Battalion by G.O.C. 25th Division	
	10		" " " Battalion by G. attack	
	11		" " " Battalion "	
	12		" " " Church Parade. Battalion training	
	13		" " " 17th Posh Push	
	14		Battalion march to BONNIERES on the way to fourth army area	

Y.20

Army Form C. 2118

WAR DIARY
or
INTELLIGENCE SUMMARY
(Erase heading not required.)

Instructions regarding War Diaries and Intelligence Summaries are contained in F.S. Regs., Part II. and the Staff Manual respectively. Title Pages will be prepared in manuscript.

Place	Date	Hour	Summary of Events and Information	Remarks and references to Appendices
ACTIVE SERVICE	June 15th		Bn billets at BONNIERES Company training	
	16th		" " " " "	
	17th		Battalion march to LONGUEVILLETTE	
	18th		" " " PERNOIS Company training	
	19th		Bn billets at PERNOIS " "	
	20th		" " " " Battalion "	
	21st		" " " " " "	
	22nd		" " " " " "	
	23rd		" " " " " "	
	24th		Battalion march to BENEVIL	
	25th		Bn billets at BENEVIL	
	26th		" " " " Company training	
	27th		Battalion march to PUNCHEVILLERS	
	28th		Bn billets at PUNCHEVILLERS " "	
	29th		" " " " " "	
	30th		Battalion marched to VARENNES	

S. Savage .... LIEUT. COL.
COMMANDING 3rd WORCESTERSHIRE REGT.

7th Bde.
25th Div.

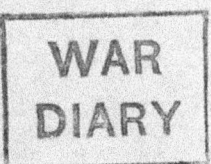

3rd BATTALION

WORCESTERSHIRE REGIMENT.

JULY 1916.

Appendices = Orders, Congratulatory Orders, Casualties.

Army Form C. 2118

WAR DIARY
or
INTELLIGENCE SUMMARY
(Erase heading not required.)

VOLUME XXIII

1916

Vol 2

Place	Date	Hour	Summary of Events and Information	Remarks and references to Appendices
July	1st		Battalion in billets at VARRENES	
	2nd		" marched to HEDAUVILLE and then on to assembly trenches in AVELUY WOOD	
	3rd		Battalion in AVELUY WOOD	
	4th		" " "	
	5th		Battalion moved up to defences in AUTHUILE and then at 12 Noon C & D companies took over original front line trenches opposite LIEPSIC Salient, A & B companies remaining in AUTHUILE defences. During the night A & D companies moved up to the LIEPSIC Salient in support to 1st WILTSHIRE Regiment, who had made an attack and were heavily counter-attacked by the enemy, who were driven off.	
	6th		A & B companies were relieved on the LIEPSIC Salient but had to go up again in support of 1st WILTSHIRE Regiment	
	7th		C & D companies moved up to the LIEPSIC Salient o relieved the 1st WILTSHIRE Regt together with the 8th LOYAL NORTH LANCS. Regt. At about 12 Midnight a battalion of the WEST YORKS took over the Salient and A & B companies moved to CRUCIFIX CORNER.	L. 2

M.S. Gills........ LIEUT. COL.
COMMANDING 3rd WORCESTERSHIRE REGT.

WAR DIARY
or
INTELLIGENCE SUMMARY
(Erase heading not required.)

Army Form

Instructions regarding War Diaries and Intelligence Summaries are contained in F. S. Regs., Part II. and the Staff Manual respectively. Title Pages will be prepared in manuscript.

Place	Date	Hour	Summary of Events and Information	Remarks and references to Appendices
	July 8th		By 11 AM the Battalion was in AVELUY WOOD trenches and moved to USNA HILL at night	
	9th		Battalion at USNA HILL in bivouacs; moved up to LA BOISSELLE and relieved the 13th Cheshire Regt.	
	10th		In trenches at LA BOISSELLE. 8th LOYAL NORTH LANCS Regt. were attacked during the night and 100 bombers were sent up in support	
	11th		In trenches at LA BOISSELLE. Heavy shelling by enemy nearly all day & night	
	12th		In trenches at LA BOISSELLE	
	13th		" " " " C Company moved up to point X 9.6.6 (Map 57DSE)	Lt. Col. J.M.C Desidbye was wounded on 13th entrusted Major W.B. Gibbs took Command of the Battalion
	14th		Battalion moved up to point X 9.6.6 where for the next three days they were in touch with the enemy found about OVILLERS. Patrols were sent out towards POSIERES and the trenches in the vicinity of point were consolidated	
	15th			
	16th			

W.S.J.W...... LIEUT. COL.
COMMANDING 3rd WORCESTERSHIRE REGT.

1875. Wt. W593/826 1,000,000 4/15 J.B.C. & A. A.D.S.S./Forms/C. 2118.

WAR DIARY
or
INTELLIGENCE SUMMARY

(Erase heading not required.)

Army Form C. 2118

Place	Date	Hour	Summary of Events and Information	Remarks and references to Appendices
	July 17th		Battalion relieved from the trenches by the 7th Warwicks and marched to FORCEVILLE, where it was billetted for the night	
	18th		Battalion march to BEAUVAL	
	19th		" in billets at BEAUVAL	
	20th		Battalion marched to AUTHIE and remained in	
	21st		" " "	
	22nd		" " "	
	23rd		Battalion marched to MAILLY WOOD. Relieving of the 29th Division being undertaken by the 25th Division	
	24th		Battalion in Divisional Reserve in MAILLY WOOD	
	25th		" " " "	
	26th		" " " "	
	27th		" " " "	
	28th		" " " "	
	29th		Battalion relieved 10th Machine Regt from trenches N E of HAMEL. W.S. White	

LIEUT. COMMANDING 3rd WORCESTERSHIRE

Reserve Army
G.A. 31/4/1.

25th Division G. 22/88

RESERVE ARMY SPECIAL ORDER.

The Commander of the Reserve Army wishes to express to the 25th and 32nd Divisions his high appreciation of the excellent work which they have done while under his command. They have been engaged day and night against a brave and determined enemy, who has had every advantage of ground, and by their perserverance and endurance they have done much to facilitate the task of the troops on their right. Progress has been steady, and the results achieved have been of great value to our cause. These Divisions are about to rest and refit and the Army Commander trusts that they will soon be ready to resume active operations.

Hd. Qrs.,
Reserve Army,
16th July, 1916.

Sgd.　N. MALCOLM, Major General,
　　　　　　　　　　General Staff.

2.

7th Infantry Bde.
74th Infantry Bde.
75th Infantry Bde.
C.R.A., 25th Div.
C.R.E., 25th Div.
O.C., 6th Bn. S.W.B.
O.C., 25th Div. Sig. Co.
O.C., 25th Div. Train
A.D.M.S.
A.A.& Q.M.G.
----

1. Forwarded for your information and communication to all troops under your command.

　　　　　　　　　　　Major,
　　　　　　　　　General Staff,
　　　　　　　　　25th Division.

17/7/16.

SPECIAL DIVISIONAL ORDER.

The G.O.C. wishes to congratulate the Wiltshire Regiment and the Worcestershire Regiment on their gallant behaviour during the operations which took place between the 6th and 8th July.

During this period the 1st Battalion Wiltshire Regiment successfully carried out 2 attacks, repelled several sustained and determined counter-attacks on 2 consecutive nights and firmly held the position won under an intense bombardment, which lasted over 4 hours.

He greatly regrets the death of Lieut-Colonel W.S.BROWN, who was killed on 6th July, whilst conducting the first attack, the success of which was greatly due to the careful preliminary arrangements made by him.

The command of the Battalion then passed to Captain S.S. OGILVIE, under whom on the night of the 6th/7th, the Battalion successfully repelled all enemy counter-attacks.

Here Lieut: R.J.A.PALMER (Wounded) and C.C.M.LESTER (Killed) behaved with the greatest gallantry.

On the July 7th, Captain Ogilvie sent Captain RUSSELL to take command of the advanced trenches and the fact that all further enemy attacks throughout the day proved a failure, was due greatly to the coolness and resource displayed by this officer.

Counter-attacks delivered during the night 7th/8th July were easily repulsed with heavy enemy losses.

At 6.30 a.m. on July 8th a second attack was organised and was launched about 8.30 a.m. under the command of Lieut: GOSDEN (Killed).

The moment the men of the Wiltshire Regiment appeared over the parapets they were met by an overwhelming fire from machine guns and rifles, but despite their many casualties, they pressed on and at 9.30 a.m. the trench which was the objective had been successfully captured and consolidated.

This performance was all the more creditable owing to the fact that the weather conditions were bad, the ground was much cut up by shell fire and the troops fatigued by the strenuous time they had gone through in the previous 36 hours.

Headquarters,
25th Division.
17th July, 1915.

A. & Q.M.G., 25th Division.
Lieut-Colonel.

As the attacking troops reached the enemy's trench the Germans were soon to bolt down the communication trenches. Large numbers were killed and 23 prisoners were taken.

It was not possible to penetrate further the enemy's communication trenches, owing to the strongly made blocks and barricades previously erected.

2/Lieut: CLEGG (since wounded), the only Officer then left, showed conspicuous ability in conducting the consolidation of the captured trench. This trench sustained a very heavy bombardment afterwards and though the cover was indifferent due to parapets being flattened by shell fire, the position was held with great determination.

The moment was now critical and the 1st Wiltshire Regiment was reinforced by 2 Companies of the 3rd Worcesters, which had been placed at the disposal of the O.C., 1st Wilts.

These companies behaved with the greatest gallantry and dash. They brought up plenty of ammunition and a large supply of bombs and with their assistance all enemy attempts at counter-attack were easily repulsed.

The work performed by 2/Lieut: HARRISON with the Trench Mortar Battery was most effective. During the 30 seconds intense bombardment preceding the assault, his guns fired no fewer than 100 rounds with great accuracy, putting out of action an enemy machine gun.

These successes could not have been obtained without the very magnificent support given by the Artillery group under Lieut-Colonel COTTON, R.F.A..

But above all they could not have been obtained except for the heroic courage, stamina and devotion to duty of the Officers, N.C.Os and men of the 1st Bn. Wiltshire and 3rd Bn. Worcestershire Regiment, so many of whom have earned undying honour by giving their lives in their country's cause.

-2-

SPECIAL DIVISIONAL ORDER.

From the 5th to the 16th July the 25th Division took the leading part in the successful operations which culminated in the capture of OVILLERS LA BOISELLE.

The village was defended with the utmost courage and determination by a garrison which consisted of some of the enemy's finest troops.

Every Battalion in the Division took part in these operations.

The Medium Trench Mortar Batteries of the Division were attached to other formations and took part in heavy fighting.

The G.O.C. has been very gratified to learn that the three batteries were all highly commended by the commanders of the formations to which they were attached.

From the many acts of gallantry that were performed, it has been possible to select only a limited number to represent to higher authority for recognition.

The following is a list of those selected by G.O.C., 25th Division -

R. F. A.

A. Battery, 110th Brigade.

```
T/Capt:    A. Anderton.
Lieut:     C.E.L. Lyne.
Cpl:       S. Broughton.
```

X/25 T.M.B. attached 110th Brigade.

```
T/Lieut:   G.B. Williams.
```

Y/25 T.M.B. attached to 111th Brigade.

```
2/Lieut:      H. Burke-Jacklin.
1786.Cpl:     J.G. Burton.
```

7th Infantry Brigade.

1st Batt: Wiltshire Regiment.

```
Lieut:     H.L.G. Hughes (R.A.M.C. attached).
  "        G.H. Penruddocke.
  "        R.J.A. Palmer.
  "(T/Capt:)G.B. Russell.
2/Lieut:      E.C. Clegg.

10950.Pte:    T. Anderson.
11070.Cpl:    D.H. Hansell.
 9313.Sgt:    W.G. Thomas.
 8490. "      G.B. Hillings.
  152.Pte:    J. Bill.
```

(continued).

7th Infantry Brigade.

1st Batt: Wiltshire Regiment.

7195.	Pte:		J. Sharpe.
7080.	"		S. Miles.
9079.	Cpl:		H. Prosser.
10750.	Pte:		W. Frost.
10 .	"	(L/C)	C. French.
7194.	"	"	W. Birch.
10412.	"		W. Bullings.
10542.	"	"	H.F. Wiltshire.
10591.	"	"	D. Smith.
5644.	"	"	J. Bird.
10962.	"		L. Guest.
10159.	"	"	G. Noble.
10070.	Cpl:		G. Gibbs.

3rd Batt: Worcestershire Regiment.

    Capt: K. Spiers.
    Lieut: J. Mould.
2/Lieut:(T/Capt:)J.B.Barron.

9275.	Pte:		M. Sullivan.
15291.	"	(L/C)	W. Bradley.
11493.	Cpl:		A. Clarke.
9945.	Sgt:		C. Price.
8467.	Pte:		A. Clewley.
10204.	"		H. Allen.
10355.	"		G. Cooper.
8234.	"		F. Banner.
10244.	Sgt:		F. Lamb.
14513.	"		F. Morrow.

10th Batt: Cheshire Regiment.

2/Lieut: H.J. Goss.
Pte: R. Ambler.
" (L/C) A. Hathers.
Sgt: J.W. Horton.

8th Battn: Loyal North Lancashire Regiment.

Major   F.G. Byrne.
Lieut: S. Ramsay.
2/Lieut: A. Harrison.

15255.	Pte:	T. Nuttall.
15772.	Sgt:	H. Holmes.

7th Company Machine Gun Corps.

12035. Pte: F. Scott.

(continued).

-4-

75th Infantry Brigade.

11th Batt: Cheshire Regiment.

24159.Pte:	A. White.	
15453.Cpl:	G. Marsden.	

2nd Batt: South Lancashire Regiment.

2/Lieut:	S.S. Jones.	
"	W. McEwan.	
8821.Pte;	J. Polglaze.	
7763.Cpl:	J. Parker.	
8538.Sgt:	F. Champion.	
10949.L/C:	H. Eden.	
13212.Pte:	J. Freeman.	
13468. "	E. Slade.	
7995.Sgt:	G. Caldicott.	

8th Batt: South Lancashire Regiment.

Capt:	G.L. Grimsdell.	
Lieut:	A. Reade.	
15269.Pte:	E. Chandler.	

R.T.F. Legge.

8/7/1916.

Lieut-Colonel,
A.A. & Q.M.G., 25th Division.

74th Infantry Brigade.

2nd Royal Irish Rifles.

	Lieut:(T/Capt)	G.W. Calverley.
	Lieut:	C.F. Wilkins.
7214.	Sgt:	G. Davies.
9341.	Cpl:	G.A. Reading.

11th Lancashire Fusiliers.

2/Lieut:	A.H. Callaghan.
L/C:	W. White.
Pte:	E. Roberts.
"	H. Thomas.

9th Batt: Loyal North Lancashire Regiment.

2/Lieut:	J. Gilroy.
"	L.H. Lanham.
"	E.U. Green.
C.S.M.	J.P. Cliff.
L/C:	F. Manning.
"	J. Hason.
Pte:	N. Nelson.

13th Batt: Cheshire Regiment.

A/Sgt:	W. Hughes.
"	J.G. Carroll.
L/C:	J. Hulme.
"	J.W. Foster.
Pte:	W. Frost.
Sgt:	R. Hayes.
Pte:	J. Webster.
"	G.T. Cain.

75th Infantry Brigade.

8th Batt: Border Regiment.

	Capt:	T.D. Hiller.
8/14777.	L/C:	W.H. Hyde.
8/15005.	"	F. Wallace.
8/20045.	Pte:	W. Yelton.
8/14544.	"	F. Roberts.
8/18049.	"	J.W. Little.
8/15181.	"	J.W. Downie.
8/15965.	Cpl:	E. Waugh.
8/18286.	"	T. Raine.
8/17234.	Pte:	W. Tidman.
8/10535.	Sgt:	E. Smart.
	Lieut:	J.E. Stewart.
	"	G.C. Hutton.

(continued).

"A" Form. Army Form C. 2121.
MESSAGES AND SIGNALS.   No. of Message

Prefix	Code	m	Words	Charge	This message is on a/c of:	Recd. at	m
Office of Origin and Service Instructions.			Sent			Date	
			At	m	Service.	From	
			To				
			By		(Signature of "Franking Officer.")	By	

TO   3/ Worcs Regt

| Sender's Number. | Day of Month | In reply to Number | AAA |
| *BM 514 | 17th | | |

Following received from 10th Corps,
begins aaa Please convey to the
25th Division the Army Commanders
thanks for their splendid work in
OVILLERS aaa ends aaa for your
information

From   7th Inf Bde
Place
Time   4.50 pm

The above may be forwarded as now corrected.   (Z)   A C Johnston Major
Censor.   Signature of Addressee or person authorised to telegraph in his name.
* This line should be erased if not required.   Bde Major

Raids carried out by
Casualties of Jogjakarta.

Date	Officers		Other Ranks			
	K	W	K	W	K	W
1 July					7	
3		1		2	19	
6		1		3	24	2
7	1	3	1(84)	14	97	13
8						
9						
10		3		6	15	9
11		1		3	37	10
12					6	-
13		1		10	22	
14				1	9	
15		1			5	-
16	1	1			8	1
17				7	40	3
Total	6	8	1	46	289	38

7th Brigade.
25th Division.

3rd BATTALION

WORCESTERSHIRE REGIMENT

AUGUST 1 9 1 6

Appendices attached:-

Report on Operations 24/25th.
Casualty Return.

Army Form C. 2118

WAR DIARY
or
INTELLIGENCE SUMMARY
(Erase heading not required.)

3 Warwick
Vol 24

Place	Date	Hour	Summary of Events and Information	Remarks and references to Appendices
ACTIVE SERV	August 1916 1		Battn in trenches opposite BEAUMONT-HAMEL	
	2		" " " " " "	
	3		" " " " " "	
	4		" " " " " "	
	5		" " " " " "	
	6		Battn relieved from trenches by 1st West Yorks 6th Division and marched to billets at BERTRANCOURT	
	7		Battn in billets at BERTRANCOURT	
	8		" " " "	
	9		" " " "	
	10		" " " "	
	11		Battn marched to SARTON	
	12		Battalion inspected by H M King George V at SARTON	27.22
	13		" " " SARTON	
	14		" " "	

COMMANDING 3rd WORCESTERSHIRE REGT. LIEUT. COL.

WAR DIARY
or
INTELLIGENCE SUMMARY

Army Form C. 2118

Place	Date August	Hour	Summary of Events and Information	Remarks and references to Appendices
BERTRANCOURT	1		Battn in trenches opposite BEAUMONT HAMEL	
	2		"	
	3		"	
	4		"	
	5		"	
	6		Battn relieved from trenches by 1st West Yorks & 4th Division and marched to billets at BERTRANCOURT.	
	7		Battn in billets at BERTRANCOURT.	
	8		"	
	9		"	
	10		"	
	11		Battn marched to SARTON	
	12		Battalion inspected by H.M. King George V at SARTON	
	13		" at SARTON	
	14		"	

.... LIEUT. COL.
COMMANDING 3rd WORCESTERSHIRE REGT.

Army Form C. 2118

WAR DIARY
or
INTELLIGENCE SUMMARY

(Erase heading not required.)

Instructions regarding War Diaries and Intelligence Summaries are contained in F. S. Regs., Part II. and the Staff Manual respectively. Title Pages will be prepared in manuscript.

Place	Date AUGUST	Hour	Summary of Events and Information	Remarks and references to Appendices
A S	15th		Battn moved to PUNCHVILLERS	
	16th		" at PUNCHVILLERS	
	17th		Battn moved to HEDAVILLE	
	18th		Battn moved to trenches near LIEPSIG SALIENT and relieved the West Yorks Regt.	
	19th		Battn in trenches near LIEPSIG SALIENT	
	20th		" " " " "	
	21st		" " " " "	
	22nd		" " " " "	
	23rd		Battalion relieved 4th Gloucesters Regt on the LIEPSIG SALIENT	
	24th		" attacked and captured German trenches ✕	✕ Accounts attached
	25th		Germans made a counter attack but were repulsed	
	26th		Battalion relieved from trenches by 8th BORDER Regiment	
	27th		" at HEDAVILLE	
	28th		" moved to bivouacs near BOUZINCOURT	
	29th			

.... LIEUT. COL.
COMMANDING 3rd WORCESTERSHIRE REGT.

Army Form C. 2118

WAR DIARY
or
INTELLIGENCE SUMMARY
(Erase heading not required.)

Instructions regarding War Diaries and Intelligence Summaries are contained in F. S. Regs., Part II. and the Staff Manual respectively. Title Pages will be prepared in manuscript.

Place	Date	Hour	Summary of Events and Information	Remarks and references to Appendices
A S	August 15th		Battn moved to PUNCHVILLERS	
	16th		" at PUNCHVILLERS	
	17th		Battn moved to HEDAVILLE	
	18th		Battn moved to trenches near LIEPSIG SALIENT and relieved the West Yorks Regt.	
	19th		Battn in trenches near LIEPSIG SALIENT	
	20th		"	
	21st		"	
	22nd		"	
	23rd		Battalion relieved 4th Gloucester Regt. in the LIEPSIG SALIENT	
	24th		" attacked and captured German trenches	Accombatted
	25th		" made a second attack but was repulsed	
	26th		Battalion relieved from trenches by 8th BORDER Regiment	
	27th		" at HEDAVILLE	
	28th		" moved to bivouacs near BOUZINCOURT	
	29th			

LIEUT. COL.
COMMANDING 3rd WORCESTERSHIRE REGT.

25th Divn.
G 472.

C.R.A. 25th Divl Artillery.
C.R.A. 48th   "   "
C.R.A. 49th   "   "
7th Infantry Brigade.
74th Infantry Brigade.
75th Infantry Brigade.
C.R.E. 25th Division.
6th S.W. Borderers
O.C. 25th Divn Signals.
O.C. 25th Divl Train.
A.D.M.S.
"Q"

The following telegram has been received from II Corps:-

" Following from Reserve Army aaa Please inform 25th Division that the Army Commander is very much pleased by the capture of the HINDENBURG Trench aaa He is particularly glad to hear that the casualties are slight aaa This shews that the preparations were thorough and reflects great credit on all concerned aaa Ends "

The Divisional Commander wishes particularly to congratulate the 3rd Battalion Worcestershire Regiment, 1st Bn Wiltshire Regiment and Royal Artillery for their excellent work.

E. M. Birch

Lieut. Colonel,
General Staff, 25th Division.

25/8/16.

Report on Operations
3rd Worcestershire

Hd. Qrs. 7th Bde.

On the morning of the 23rd the Battalion took over trenches R 31 b 90 — 62 and X 1 a 79 — X 1 b 91, the 1st Wilts being on our left and 1st Bucks of 48th Division on our right.

At 4.10 p.m. on 24th the battalion advanced to attack on trench 26-35-64 and was completely successful, the ground gained on right exceeding objective and point R 31 d 74 was reached and a barricade erected. Owing to the advance being carried out very close behind our barrage no difficulty was experienced in crossing No Mans Land, practically the only casualties being caused by our own barrage owing to some men going too far ahead. The enemy found our men on top of them before they could man the parapet or get their machine guns into action. The enemy offered a stout resistance in the trench and here most of my casualties occurred in bomb fighting. The enemy suffered severely, the whole of a machine gun detachment which tried to get their gun on parapet at Point 64 were shot down by one of my Lewis Guns which was very quickly brought up on to a traverse and did great execution down the trench. The enemy bombed inwards vigorously from direction of Point 94 and down trench from NORTH at Point 35, but his bombing parties were destroyed or driven back within half an hour. Barricades were formed at these points and the enemy abandoned the position.

Trench mortar and smoke bombs were flung down entrances of dugouts and a considerable number of enemy were destroyed in certainly 2 dugouts by these bombs, remainder surrendering; about 80 prisoners, including wounded, being taken.

The position was completely in our hands by 5.30 p.m. Two machine guns were captured and large numbers of rifles, equipment and bombs. The Wilts Regt. gained their objective on the left and communication was established at Point 81 by a joint post with 1st Bucks Regt.

The captured position was extensively damaged by our shell fire and practically no fire trench remained. Consolidation was pushed on at once and all night, a strong post with Lewis Gun being built at Point 94. The captured machine guns were also erected on the parapet and made use of, a good supply of ammunition being captured. Two guns of 4th M.G. Coy were also established in my front.

The enemy made no effort to attack during the night, but patrols approached at dawn on 25th inst., one of whom was shot within 50 yards of my line.

The captured position was shelled heavily during afternoon of 25th and at 5.30 p.m. the whole of the sector occupied by the Battalion was bombarded intensely, the enemy massing in his trenches for the attack. He endeavoured to get on to the parapet but immediately came under our machine gun fire and shortly after our Artillery barrage was brought on to his line in R 31 d, which completely stopped his attack. One of my men actually went on to the enemy's parapet at about 7.30 p.m. and found him still standing to in the trenches with fixed bayonets. All attempts to attack completely failed and the enemy was unable to approach my parapet owing to the accuracy of our Artillery fire.

Beyond continual and heavy shelling

of sector held by battalion the situation remained unchanged until battalion was relieved on 26th inst.

27/8/16

M S Gibbs Lt Col
O.C. 3/Worc. Regt.

Casualties from 1st August to 26th August 1916.

Date	Officers K	W	M	Total	Other Ranks K	W	M	Total	Remarks
1st Aug 1916					5	1		6	Officer casualties
2nd "						1		1	Killed 2/Lt w.L. Perks
3rd "					1	8		9	
4th "						1		1	Wounded
5th "					2	5		7	Major Briscoe
6th "		1		1	1	8		9	Capt. Akers
19th "						1		1	" Barron (at duty)
20th "						10		10	
21st "		1		1	2	4		6	Lieut Lazarus
22nd "		1		1	7	49		56	2/Lt Rundle
23rd "		1		1	24	123	11	158	" Lee
24th "	1	5		6	9	34	1	44	" Kilby
25th "					4	13	3	20	" Sharpe
26th "									
Totals	1	8		9	55	266	15	336	

7th. INFANTRY BDE.

25th. DIVISION

3rd. WORCESTER REGT.

S E P T E M B E R 1 9 1 6.

WAR DIARY
or
INTELLIGENCE SUMMARY

Army Form C. 2118

B.M. Worcester R Vol 25

1916

J.23

Place	Date	Hour	Summary of Events and Information	Remarks and references to Appendices
ACTIVE SERVICE	August 30th		Battn in bivouac near BOUZINCOURT	
	31st		" " " " "	
	SEPTEMBER			
	1		" " " " "	
	2		Bn moved up to dugouts near BLACK HORSE BRIDGE near AUTHUILLE.	
	3		Bn attacked German trenches R31C45 – R31A30 (Mly.Ref. 57 D.S.E.) The trenches were gained by A & B Companies but owing to the heavy enemy shelling for [?] had to be evacuated. Casualties were severe. Bn were relieved by the 10th Cheshire Regt and moved to bivouacs near BOUZINCOURT.	
	4			
	5		Bn marched to hutments in ACHEUX	
	6		Bn marched to billets in ARQUEVES	
	7		Bn at ARQUEVES	
	8		" " "	
	9		" " "	
	10		Bn march to billets in GAIZINCOURT	

P.W. Willa...... LIEUT. COL.
COMMANDING 3rd WORCESTERSHIRE REGT

Army Form C. 2118

WAR DIARY
or
INTELLIGENCE SUMMARY
(Erase heading not required.)

Instructions regarding War Diaries and Intelligence Summaries are contained in F. S. Regs., Part II. and the Staff Manual respectively. Title Pages will be prepared in manuscript.

Place	Date	Hour	Summary of Events and Information	Remarks and references to Appendices
ACTIVE SERVICE	SEPTEMBER 11		Bn at GAIZINCOURT	
	12		Bn marched to PROUVILLE	
	13		Bn marched to MAISON-ROLLANDS	
	14		Bn at MAISON-ROLLANDS	
	15		" " "	
	16		" " "	
	17		" " "	
	18		" " "	
	19		" " "	
	20		" " "	
	21		" " "	
	22		" " "	
	23		" " "	
	24		" " "	
	25		Bn marched to GAIZINCOURT	
	26		" " to ARQUEVES	

Prouville

Army Form C. 2118

WAR DIARY
or
INTELLIGENCE SUMMARY

(Erase heading not required.)

Instructions regarding War Diaries and Intelligence Summaries are contained in F. S. Regs., Part II. and the Staff Manual respectively. Title Pages will be prepared in manuscript.

Place	Date	Hour	Summary of Events and Information	Remarks and references to Appendices
ACTIVE SERVICE	SEPTEMBER 27th		Bn at ARQUEVES	
	28th		" "	
	29th		Bn marched to HEDAUVILLE.	

7th INFANTRY BDE.

25th DIVISION.

3rd BATTALION.

WORCESTERSHIRE REGIMENT.

OCTOBER 1916

Army Form C. 2118

Vol 26
3 Worcesters

WAR DIARY
or
INTELLIGENCE SUMMARY
(Erase heading not required.)

1916

J.24

Place	Date	Hour	Summary of Events and Information	Remarks and references to Appendices
ACTIVE SERVICE	SEPTEMBER 30th		Bn moved up to the original German front line north of OVILLERS into Brigade Reserve, the Brigade relieving the 33rd Brigade 11th Div.	
	OCTOBER 1st		Bn in Brigade Reserve	
	2nd		" relieved the 8th L.N. LANCS Regiment from the Left Sector of Brigade front- line in HESSIAN TRENCH. 1st WILTSHIRE Regt. on right and 55th Brigade (18th Division) on Left. Bn. from R20D91 to R20 D15.	
	3rd		Bn in trenches	
	4th		" " "	
	5th		" " "	
	6th		" " 1st WILTS. Regiment relieved by 10th CHESHIRE Regiment	
	7th		" " 10th CHESHIRE Regiment relieved by 8th L.N. LANCS. Regiment	
	8th		" " 8th L.N. LANCS Regiment relieved by 10th CHESHIRE Regiment	
	9th		" who successfully captured and consolidated the Northern portion of the STUFF REDOUBT	
	10th		Bn in front line trenches	

Lieut. Col.
COMMANDING 3rd WORCESTERSHIRE REGT.

Army Form C. 2118

WAR DIARY
or
INTELLIGENCE SUMMARY

(Erase heading not required.)

Instructions regarding War Diaries and Intelligence Summaries are contained in F.S. Regs., Part II. and the Staff Manual respectively. Title Pages will be prepared in manuscript.

Place	Date	Hour	Summary of Events and Information	Remarks and references to Appendices
ACTIVE SERVICE	OCTOBER 11th		Bn in front trenches. 10th CHESHIRE Regiment relieved by 8th L.N. LANCS Regiment.	
	12th		Bn relieved by the 1st WILTS. Regiment from front line and moved into support in the DANUBE, CONSTANCE and JOSEPH. TRENCHES. B Company in support to 8th L.N. LANCS in ZOLLERN TRENCH.	
	13th		Bn in support trenches.	
	14th	"	8th L.N. LANCS Regiment captured and consolidated the MOUNDS north of STUFF. REDOUBT.	
	15th	"	Bn relieved by 8th S. LANCS Regiment (75th Brigade) and marched to bivouacs near BOUZINCOURT.	
	16th	"	Bn moved up to the dug-outs at CRUCIFIX CORNER (near AVELUY) and relieved 10th CHESHIRE Regiment.	
	17th	"	Bn at CRUCIFIX CORNER 7th Brigade lent to the 74th and 75th Brigades for working and carrying parties in the forward area.	
	18th	"	" " " "	
	19th	"	" " " "	
	20th	"	" " " "	

PRWKelly LIEUT COL
COMMANDING 8th [LOYAL NORTH LANCASHIRE] REGT

Army Form C. 2118

WAR DIARY
or
INTELLIGENCE SUMMARY
(Erase heading not required.)

Instructions regarding War Diaries and Intelligence Summaries are contained in F. S. Regs., Part II. and the Staff Manual respectively. Title Pages will be prepared in manuscript.

Place	Date	Hour	Summary of Events and Information	Remarks and references to Appendices
ACTIVE SERVICE	OCTOBER 21st		Bn at CRUCIFIX CORNER. Successful attack on the REGINA and STUFF trenches by the 74th and 75th Brigades.	
	22nd		Bn relieved by the 6th WILTS Regiment (19th Division) and marched to Stables in BOUZINCOURT	
	23rd		Bn marched to HERISSART	
	24th		" " " LONGUEVILLETTE	
	25th		Bn in billets at "	
	26th		" " " "	
	27th		" " " "	
	28th		" " " "	
	29th		Bn entrained for second army area at DOULLENS and detrained at BAILLEUL about 3.30 A M on the 30th	
	30th		Bn marched from BAILLEUL Station to OOSTROHOVE FARM	
	31st		Bn at OOSTROHOVE FARM.	

1875 Wt. W593/826 1,000,000 4/15 J.B.C. & A. A.D.S.S./Forms/C. 2118.

3rd Bn Worcestershire Regt

Casualties for 3rd September 1916

Officers			Other Ranks			Remarks
K	W	M	K	W	M	
7	–	–	11	72	11	Officers Killed:— Lt Col W B Cubitt; Capt J Mould; " J King; Lieut J W Lerrell (Glouc Regt); 2/Lieut H G Bernard —"—; " R S Jones; " A C G Alford (Glouc)

3rd Bn Middlesex Regt

Casualties for 3rd September 1916

Officers			Other Ranks			Remarks
K	W	M	K	W	M	
4	-	-	11	72	11	Officers killed —
Lt Col W.B.Lubbs
Capt J Mould
H Third
Lieut Sir Lowell I Gun Regt
2Lieut H.C.Bernard
K.A.Jones
O.C.G Alpro/Gloue.

Casualties October 1916

Date	Officers K	Officers W	Officers M	Other Ranks K	Other Ranks W	Other Ranks M	Total
3				3	3		3
4					8		8
5		1.			12		13
6				5	14	5	24
7					2		2
8					7		7
9				4	10		24
10				3	3		3
11				2	4		7
12				1	11		12
13					9		10
14					4	1	5
15							
16							
17				1	1		1
18					4		5
Total		1.		27	92	6.	125.

Lieut. J W Luby

P. Walker

7th INFANTRY BDE.

25th DIVISION.

3rd BATTALION.

WORCESTERSHIRE REGIMENT

NOVEMBER 1916

Army Form C. 2118

WAR DIARY
or
INTELLIGENCE SUMMARY
(Erase heading not required.)

3rd Worcestershire Regt.

Vol 27

1916

1/25

L.25

Place	Date	Hour	Summary of Events and Information	Remarks and references to Appendices
ACTIVE SERVICE	NOVEMBER 1st		Battalion relieved 9th Devon Regt. 7th Devon Regt trenches in LE TOUQUET sector east of LE BIZET. Battalion right on LYS and left on ESSEX FARM. (Map Ref HOUPLINES Sheet 36.N.W. 1/10000). 2nd New Zealand Brigade on right on 10th Cheshire Regt on left.	
	2nd		Battalion in trenches	
	3rd		" " "	
	4th		" " "	
	5th		" " "	
	6th		" " "	
	7th		Battalion relieved by 8th Loyal North Lancs Regt from trenches and moved to Brigade Support in LE BIZET. 2 Companies and 1 Platoon garrisoning the supporting trenches, remainder of Battalion in LE BIZET.	
	8th		Battalion in Brigade Support	
	9th		" " " "	
	10th		" " " "	

1875 Wt. W593/326 1,000,000 4/15 J.B.C. & A. A.D.S.S./Forms/C. 2118.

Army Form C. 2118

WAR DIARY
or
INTELLIGENCE SUMMARY
(Erase heading not required.)

Instructions regarding War Diaries and Intelligence Summaries are contained in F. S. Regs., Part II. and the Staff Manual respectively. Title Pages will be prepared in manuscript.

Place	Date	Hour	Summary of Events and Information	Remarks and references to Appendices
ACTIVE SERVICE	NOVEMBER 11th		Battalion in Brigade Support.	
	12th		" " " "	
	13th		Battalion relieved 8th Royal West Surrey Regt from trenches	
	14th		" in trenches	
	15th		" " "	
	16th		" " "	
	17th		" " "	
	18th		" " "	
	19th		Battalion relieved from trenches by 8th Royal West Surrey Regt and moved into Brigade Support Queens at PONT DE NIEPPE	
	20th		Battalion in Brigade Reserve	
	21st		" " " " ⎫	
	22nd		" " " " ⎬ Working parties for front line found.	
	23rd		" " " " ⎪	
	24th		" " " " ⎭	

Army Form C. 2118

WAR DIARY
or
INTELLIGENCE SUMMARY
(Erase heading not required.)

Instructions regarding War Diaries and Intelligence Summaries are contained in F. S. Regs., Part II. and the Staff Manual respectively. Title Pages will be prepared in manuscript.

Place	Date	Hour	Summary of Events and Information	Remarks and references to Appendices
ACTIVE SERVICE	NOVEMBER			
	25th		Battalion relieved 8th Royal West Surrey Regt from trenches	
	26th		" " in trenches	
	27th		" " "	
	28th		" " "	
	29th		" " "	
	30th		" " "	

P. Wahab, LIEUT. COL.
COMMANDING 3rd WORCESTERSHIRE REGT.

Casualties November 1916

Date	Officer			Other Ranks			Total O.R.
	K	W	M	K	W	M	
2 Nov 1916				4			4
3 "					2		2
27 "	—	Nil		1	3		3
29 "				1	1		2
30 "							1
Totals				6	6		12

7th INFANTRY BDE.

25th DIVISION.

3rd BATTALION.

WORCESTERSHIRE REGIMENT.

DECEMBER 1916

WAR DIARY
or
INTELLIGENCE SUMMARY

(*Erase heading not required.*)

Army Form C. 2118.

Vol 28

1926

Hour, Date, Place	Summary of Events and Information	Remarks and References to Appendices

ACTIVE SERVICE DECEMBER

1. Battalion relieved from trenches by 8 Loyal North Lancs Regt & moved into Brigade Support at
2.
3.
4.
5. LE B,ZET. 2 Companies & 1 Platoon garrisoning
6. the supporting points, remainder of Battalion
   " LE B,ZET. Battalion in Brigade Support
7. "
8. Battalion relieved 8" Loyal Lancs Regt in trenches in trenches"
9. "
10. "
11. "
12. "
13. Battalion relieved from trenches by 8th Loyal North Lancs Regt & moved in Brigade Reserve at PONT DE NIEPPE.

Army Form C. 2118.

WAR DIARY
or
INTELLIGENCE SUMMARY
(Erase heading not required.)

Instructions regarding War Diaries and Intelligence Summaries are contained in F. S. Regs, Part II. and the Staff Manual respectively. Title pages will be prepared in manuscript.

Hour, Date, Place	Summary of Events and Information	Remarks and References to Appendices
Ultra Douve DECEMBER 14	Battalion in Brigade Reserve	
15	" " " " working parties for	
16	" " " " front line trenches	
17	" " " "	
18	" " " "	
19	" " " "	
20	" " " "	
21	Battalion relieved 8 Loyal Lancs Regt from trenches	
22	" " " " in trenches	
23	" " " "	
24	" " " "	
25	" " " "	
26	" " " "	
27	Battalion relieved from trenches by 8 Loyal North Lancs Regt — moved to Brigade support at LE BIZET	
28	Battalion in Brigade Support.	

Army Form C. 2118.

WAR DIARY
or
INTELLIGENCE SUMMARY
(Erase heading not required.)

Instructions regarding War Diaries and Intelligence Summaries are contained in F. S. Regs., Part II. and the Staff Manual respectively. Title pages will be prepared in manuscript.

Hour, Date, Place	Summary of Events and Information	Remarks and References to Appendices
Active Service December 29 30 31	Battalion in Brigade support	

P. R. Whalley .... LIEUT. COL.
COMMANDING 3rd WORCESTERSHIRE REGT.

3rd Bn Worcestershire Regt.

Casualties during December 1916

Date	Officers			Other Ranks			Total
	K	W	M	K	W	M	O.R
11 Dec 1916				1	1	1	1
13 Dec 1916		Nil		1	1	1	1
17 Dec 1916				1	1	1	1
				3	3	3	3

Maude
Lieut. Col.
Commanding 3rd Worcestershire Regt.

Army Form C. 2118.

3rd BATTALION
WORCESTERSHIRE
REGIMENT.
W.O. 434
Date 3/1/17

Vol 29

J.27

WAR DIARY
or
INTELLIGENCE SUMMARY

(Erase heading not required.)

Instructions regarding War Diaries and Intelligence Summaries are contained in F. S. Regs., Part II. and the Staff Manual respectively. Title pages will be prepared in manuscript.

Hour, Date, Place		Summary of Events and Information	Remarks and References to Appendices
Active Service. January	1	Bn relieved 8' Loyal North Lancs Regt in the same trenches as before (C16 B 8.5 to C10.B.1.8)	Map Sheet 36 N.W.
"	2	Bn extended its front to the left taking over from 1st Cheshire Regt up to C.4.A.60.	
"	3 to 6.	Bn in trenches. Quiet tour.	
"	7	Bn relieved by 8" Loyal North Lancs Regt. and moved into Bde Reserve at PONT-DE-NIEPPE.	
"	8 to 12.	Bn in Brigade Reserve finding working parties daily	
"	13.	Bn relieved 8' Loyal North Lancs Regt in the trenches as before.	
"	14 to 16.	Bn in trenches. Quiet tour.	

M Walker

............................LIEUT. COL.
COMMANDING 3rd WORCESTERSHIRE REGT.

Army Form C. 2118.

WAR DIARY
or
INTELLIGENCE SUMMARY
(Erase heading not required.)

Hour, Date, Place	Summary of Events and Information	Remarks and References to Appendices
Active Service January 17 DE-NIEPPE	Bn relieved from trenches by 11th Cheshire Regt. 75th Inf. Bde and moved into Divisional Reserve at PONT-DE-NIEPPE.	
" 18631	Bn in Divisional Reserve engaged in training near NIEPPE and in training area near BAILLEUL up to 27th inst. After that time almost exclusively occupied by finding large working parties in the neighbourhood of PLOEGSTEERT WOOD and ST YVES repairing damage done by enemy bombardment. Weather very cold and frosty throughout and ground ice bound.	

.... LIEUT. COL.
COMMANDING 3rd WORCESTERSHIRE REGT.

Casualties during the month of January 1917

Date	Officers			Other Ranks			Remarks
	K	W	Total	K	W	Total	
2nd Jan: 17	-	-	-	1	2	3	
5th Jan: 17	-	-	-	-	1	1	
7th Jan: 17	-	-	-	1	1	2	
12 Jan: 17	-	-	-	-	1	1	
14 Jan: 17	-	-	-	-	1	1	
15 Jan: 17	-	-	-	-	2	2	
Totals	-	-	-	2	8	10	

31st Jan: 17

.... LIEUT. COL.
COMMANDING 3rd WORCESTERSHIRE REGT.

Army Form C. 2118.

3RD BATTALION,
WORCESTERSHIRE
REGIMENT.
W.O. 94.....
Date 22/2/17

WAR DIARY
INTELLIGENCE SUMMARY

(Erase heading not required.)

Instructions regarding War Diaries and Intelligence Summaries are contained in F. S. Regs., Part II. and the Staff Manual respectively. Title pages will be prepared in manuscript.

Hour, Date, Place	Summary of Events and Information	Remarks and References to Appendices
February 1. 1917.	Bn in Div¹ Reserve at NIEPPE.	
" 2.	Bn relieved 11th Lancashire Fusiliers in the line, between U21B6585 & U15A94. (8th LN Lancs Regt on right, 10th W Ble. 25th Div on left.)	Sheet 28 S.W.
" 3. 4. 5.	Bn in trenches. Very quiet tour. Weather very cold, hard frost continuing. Artillery & TM Bombardment of our trenches on our left not serious, no damage 4.5., about 26th no fire, practised no retaliation.	PRW.
" 6.	Bn relieved by 10th Cheshire Regt. & proceeded to Bde reserve at REGINA CAMP. (T29D)	PRW.
" 10	Bn relieved 10th Cheshire Regt. - left subsector.	
" 11. 12. 13	Trenches quiet, weather still very cold. Frost continuing.	A.9
" 14	Bn relieved by 10th Cheshire Regt & remained in Bde. support at CRESLOW FARM.	A.9
" 18	Bn. relieved 10th Cheshire Regt in left subsector. Our patrols on that evening brought in several dead & two wounded men of the 10th Cheshire Regt. left from the raid on the 17th inst	A5
" 19. 6. 21	Enemies TM active and artillery. Trenches bad owing to the thaw	A.9

F. A. Chapham Major
Command 2nd Worcestershire

WAR DIARY
or
INTELLIGENCE SUMMARY

(Erase heading not required.)

Army Form C. 2118.

Hour, Date, Place	Summary of Events and Information	Remarks and References to Appendices
February 22. 1917	Bn. relieved by 4th Bn. New Zealand Rifle Brigade & moved to billets at NIEPPE for the night.	28.
" 23	Bn. marched to ROOKLOSHILLE. Billets very scattered and training grounds scarce.	Sheet 27 S.W. 19. 15.
" 24 - 28	Bn. undergoing Training in Corps. Reserve.	

28.2.17

F. N. Chaplin Major
Comdg 3rd Worcestershire Regt.

Army Form C. 2118.

3RD BATTALION,
WORCESTERSHIRE
REGIMENT.
No. W.O. 15.16
Date 31/3/17.

WAR DIARY
or
INTELLIGENCE SUMMARY
(Erase heading not required.)

Instructions regarding War Diaries and Intelligence Summaries are contained in F. S. Regs., Part II. and the Staff Manual respectively. Title pages will be prepared in manuscript.

Hour, Date, Place	Summary of Events and Information	Remarks and References to Appendices
March 1 to 10 - 1917	Bn. in Corps Reserve at ROOKLOSHILLE, training.	Sheet 5 A (HAZEBROUCK)
11	Bn. moved to new area at EBBLINGHEM.	
12 to 18	Bn. Engaged in training round EBBLINGHEM	
19	Bn. marched to SEC-BOIS	
20	Bn. in billets at SEC-BOIS.	
21	Bn. marched to OUTTERSTEENE area.	
22	Bn. in billets at OUTTERSTEENE. 25th Bn. attached to 2nd ANZACS Corps.	
23	Bn. marched to KORTEPYP CAMP, near NEUVE EGLISE	Sheet 28
24/30	Bn. at KORTEPYP CAMP. Bn. Engaged in carrying parties in vicinity of front line	
31	Bn. marched to LA CRECHE area, near STEENWERCK.	

P W Miller
................LIEUT. COL.
COMMANDING 3rd WORCESTERSHIRE REGT.

Casualties during March 1917

Date	Officers			Other Ranks			Total	
	K.	M.	Total	K.	W.	M.		
28 March/17	Nil			-	1	-	1	Slightly still at duty
Totals				-	1	-	1	

31st March 1917.

.... LIEUT. COL
COMMANDING 3rd WORCESTERSHIRE REGT.

Army Form C. 2118.

WAR DIARY
or
INTELLIGENCE SUMMARY.

(Erase heading not required.)

Place	Date	Hour	Summary of Events and Information	Remarks and references to Appendices.
LA CRÈCHE AREA	1917 Apl 1-4		The battalion carried out tis and company training whilst in this area.	
ST MARIE CAPPEL	5		The battalion marched to ST MARIE CAPPEL, and during its stay	
	6		there underwent a course of musketry under the Supervision of the staff of 2nd Div Musketry School. During the whole period the severity of the weather was most marked	
	12			
OUTTERSTEENE	13		Battalion marched to OUTTERSTEENE era. en route to the trenches	
LE BIZET	14		Bn relieved 8th L.N. Lancashire Regt. and became battalion in Brigade support. C Co occupied the Subsidiary posts and B Co went into GRAND RABEC FARM, and were placed at the tactical disposal of the battalion commander holding the front line	
"	15	7.45 p.m	Enemy raided front line between LONG AVE. and ESSEX CENTRAL Farm. The 10th Cheshire Regt. who were holding the line called on D Co for support. D Co. moved up to STATION REDOUBT but were not required, the raid being over.	J.30

Army Form C. 2118.

WAR DIARY
or
INTELLIGENCE SUMMARY.
(Erase heading not required.)

Instructions regarding War Diaries and Intelligence Summaries are contained in F. S. Regs., Part II. and the Staff Manual respectively. Title pages will be prepared in manuscript.

Place	Date	Hour	Summary of Events and Information	Remarks and references to Appendices
	1917 April			
LE BIZET	16		A quiet day. Nothing to report	NIL
TRENCHES	17 -20		The Battalion relieved the 10th Cheshire Regt. in the LE TOUQUET Sector and held the line from the river LYS to the north end of F. Sub. A quiet and uneventful tour, except for the last day. During the relief enemy shelled vicinity of RESERVE FARM heavily with H.E. and inflicted casualties on No 2 Platoon. Six men being killed. The Battalion was relieved by 2nd South Lancs, and in relief moved back to OUTTERSTEENE AREA	
OUTTERSTEENE	21 -29		Bn formed numerous working parties for company making accoutrements dismounted etc. Practised improvement in the weather. Ground drying up rapidly.	Nil
STRAZEELE	30		Bn moved unexpectedly, and at an early hours to Billets in this area.	K.R.L.l

PRMValley, Lt. Col
Comdg 3rd Wire Rgt.

30 April, 1917.

3rd Bn Worcestershire Regt.

Casualties during April 1917

Date	Officers			Other Ranks			Total O.R.	Remarks
	K	W	M	K	W	M		
15-4-17					3		3	
19-4-17	NIL				2		2	
20-4-17				6	2		8	
				6	7		13	

P R Whalley ......LIEUT. COL.
COMMANDING 3rd WORCESTERSHIRE REGT.

3rd Worcesters 7/15

Army Form C. 2118.

WAR DIARY
or
INTELLIGENCE SUMMARY.
(Erase heading not required.)

Instructions regarding War Diaries and Intelligence Summaries are contained in F.S. Regs., Part II. and the Staff Manual respectively. Title pages will be prepared in manuscript.

Place	Date	Hour	Summary of Events and Information	Remarks and references to Appendices
STRAZEELE	1917 May 1-4		Whilst in this area training under company arrangements continued	R.A.C
AREA				
EBBLINGHEM	4		Bn. marched to EBBLINGHEM a distance of about eleven miles. Conditions of march very trying	R.A.C
ETREHEM	5		March continued to the 2nd Army training area. Bn HQ & A pl. established at ETREHEM and B Coy billeted in LEULINE and C & D at AUDENTHUN. R.A.C. Billets although somewhat scattered called quite good.	
ETREHEM	6 -13		Company training continued. Battalion training commenced. All companies had two days firing on one of the 2nd Army Range Battalion Sports held on 13th Weather was very hot.	J.B.C
	14/5		Training continued - Rifle operators on 15th	
	16/7		Bn. practised an assault on trenches. Three lines of defence had to be captured	4. 31
EBBLINGHEM	18		Bn. marched to EBBLINGHEM. Trying conditions for marching, very warm.	Wasschenbeek SA
STRAZEELE	19		Bn. marched to STRAZEELE. In division to the trenches were later	to
BAILLEUL AREA	20		Bn. marched to bivouacs at RAVELSBERG CAMP. Under canvas Pleasant encp.	S.28 S.16.d.55

T2134. Wt. W708-776. 50C000. 4/15. Sir J. C. & S.

Army Form C. 2118.

3 Worcester Regt

Vol 33

WAR DIARY
or
INTELLIGENCE SUMMARY.
(Erase heading not required.)

Place	Date	Hour	Summary of Events and Information	Remarks and references to Appendices
BAILLEUL AREA	1917 May 21-23		Bn found large working parties for unloading, carrying ammunition, building dumps &c	S.28 T 19.b.70
	24		Bn relieved the 13th Cheshire Regt at ALDERSHOT CAMP	
NEUVE EGLISE	24-26		Bn found working parties for digging & repairing trenches in the WULVERGHEM sector. 7th Inf Brigade relieved 74th Inf Brigade in this sector.	
			Bn in Brigade Reserve	
	29		Bn marched to Entrances in a field at T.1.d.2.8	S.28
	30-31		Bn found working parties mainly in the vicinity of the front line. About 300 men assisted in digging a new front line trench, 150 yds from the enemy trenches, in preparation for offensive action. Our casualties 1 killed 4 wounded (this at Bulls). The trench was successfully excavated.	
	31st May 1917			

Preville
Lt. Col.
Comdg. 3rd Worcestershire Regt.

Casualties for month of May 1917

WO 413

Date	Officers	Other Ranks				Remarks
		K.	W.	M	Total	
26th May '17		-	1	-	1.	Includes 4 OR
27" " "	NIL	-	1	-	1.	wounded slightly at
29 " "		-	2	-	2.	duty.
30 " "		1	4	-	5.	
		1.	8	-	9.	

P. K. .... LIEUT. COL.
COMMANDING 3rd WORCESTERSHIRE REGT.

WAR DIARY or INTELLIGENCE SUMMARY

Army Form C. 2118.

2/8 3rd Bn Worcester Regt

Place	Date	Hour	Summary of Events and Information	Remarks and references to Appendices
NEUVE EGLISE T.1.d.2.8	1917 June 1st		Battalion in bivouacs in field, as per reference in margin, whilst here the Bn continued to find working parties in forward area and front line, in preparation for the forthcoming offensive operations. B Co rehearsed protective raid. Further rehearsal for raid by B Co.	Mess tents J.A.L.
	2	8.45 pm	B Co under the command of Lt. A. J. B. HUDSON, and accompanied by 2/Lts. S. T. DIXON and C. GREENHILL, paraded about 80 strong and marched to the trenches to carry out a raid. The object of the raid was to capture prisoners, reconnoitre the enemy's trenches and ascertain his method of holding them. The front selected for entry was 40 yds north of NUTMEG AVE N36.d.n.6 to 40 yds north of NUTMEG AVE N36.d.S.S.0. and thence along NUTMEG AVE to NUTMEG SUPPORT. In conjunction with this operation the 2 Loyal North Lancashire Regt. who were holding the front line, also made a raid at about N36.C.b	
		10.45 pm	The attacking troops found the wire in front of our trenches and trenches opposite cut in front by firing of our Lyngs.	

Army Form C. 2118.

WAR DIARY
or
INTELLIGENCE SUMMARY.
(Erase heading not required.)

Place	Date	Hour	Summary of Events and Information	Remarks and references to Appendices
TRENCHES N.36.d.15	June 7 1917	10.10pm	ZERO. Our artillery barrage was opened on the enemy's front line, and their front in rear, which lifted at zero + 2. The enemy's front line was completely entered. Some resistance was offered, which was speedily overcome by the resolution of our troops, and all the enemy encountered were either killed or taken prisoner. The advance was then continued in accordance with plan, and at zero + 7 NUTMEG SUPPORT was reached. At the junction of NUTMEG AVE and NUTMEG SUPPORT an enemy machine gun opened fire. This was immediately attacked with bombs and the team fled. No prisoners were taken on this line. Some Germans were seen running away on our rear entered. At zero + 13 our troops withdrew from our trenches, and under cover of our artillery barrage returned to our own lines. The enemy's retaliation was chiefly confined to an H.E. barrage which fell on our front line trench immediately after the zero. Just one prisoner was brought back to our trench, five others being killed crossing "no mans land", for the most part the enemy showed little inclination	

T2134. Wt. W708—776. 50000. 4/15. ST J.C.& S.

WAR DIARY
or
INTELLIGENCE SUMMARY.
(Erase heading not required.)

Army Form C. 2118.

Instructions regarding War Diaries and Intelligence Summaries are contained in F. S. Regs., Part II. and the Staff Manual respectively. Title pages will be prepared in manuscript.

Place	Date	Hour	Summary of Events and Information	Remarks and references to Appendices
	June 1917			
	2		to fight, and appeared glad to be taken. All prisoners belonged to the 181 Regt. Our casualties were 3 O.R. killed, and 10 wounded, most of whose wounds were slight. The raid was entirely successful. Congratulatory messages were received from the C of S and Divisional Commander.	O.O. 142 attached Attached Appx A.
RAVELSBURG S.17.c.1.8	3	6 a.m.	Bn. relieved by 8th South Lancashire Regt. and moved to Reserves at RAVELSBURG. The 7th Bn. was withdrawn from the Line, and handed over the 75th Inf. Bde. working parties of 200 were found for the front Line and forward area	R.N.C
		5.30 p.m.	the Divisional Chaplain of the Division held divine service for the Bn	R.A.C
	4		Continued to find working parties of 200 at 7 p.m.	R.A.C
	5		Orders received that the Bn. be would move up to the Line into positions of assembly for forthcoming offensive operations in the evening of the 6th inst. In the evening offensive situations. The C.O. had a conference of company commanders at 9 p.m.	R.A.C
	6	2.30 p.m.	A Co. left RAVELSBERG CAMP at 2.30 p.m. to take over the battalion position of assembly in the front Line trenches from N36.d.3.2 to N36.c.9.6	

T2134. Wt. W708—776. 500'000. 4/15. Sir J. C. & S.

WAR DIARY or INTELLIGENCE SUMMARY.

Army Form C. 2118.

(Erase heading not required.)

Place	Date	Hour	Summary of Events and Information	Remarks and references to Appendices
TRENCHES	June 1917 6	9.30 p.m.	The battalion started to move in position of assembly at this hour.	
ONSLOW			During assembly there was intermittent hostile shelling, but no casualties were suffered. They then had on its immediate right the 13th Cheshire Regt.	
TRENCH N.36.d.2.3.			2nd Bn Kols and on its left the 6th Royal North Lancashire Regt. Bn H.Q. was at N.36.c.95.00. During the period of waiting the men were supplied with hot tea. Men had also been served out with "Tommy Cookers" to enable them to find occasion during a coming period. The following officers went into action with the Bn:- Hd.Qr. LT.COL. P.W.HALLEY, LT.L.PIPER (ADJT), LT.C.W.HARGREAVES, and 2LT R.C.PERRY. 'A' Co. CAPT. A.BIRCH JONES, 2LTS A.V.B.ROWLANDS, R.J.R.MACKENZIE. 'B' Co. LT.A.J.B.HUDSON (comdg) 2LTS. G.W.LAZARUS, C. GREENHILL, and J.T. DIXON. 'C' Co. CAPT.I.N.MASON, 2LTS. L.M.METCALFE, and C.E.S.BRIMMELL. 'D' Co. CAPT.R.S.McDONALD, 2LTS.L.C.EVANS and F.W.BRAMPTON. 2LT E.V.P.PARSONS was in charge of a carrying party of about 80 O.R. CAPT. H.D.WILLIS R.A.M.C. and the Rev G.M.EVANS went at the Regt aid post. Strength battalion going into action 618 O.R. including carrying party of 80	

Army Form C. 2118.

WAR DIARY
or
INTELLIGENCE SUMMARY.
(Erase heading not required.)

Place	Date	Hour	Summary of Events and Information	Remarks and references to Appendices
TRENCHES N36.d.2.8	June 1917 7	3.10 a.m.	Zero hour. Under cover of the greatest weight of artillery ever employed in battle the Bn left its position of assembly, and moved forward to the assault, at the same moment many mines were sprung under the enemy front line, the assault to the battalion being at ONTARIO FARM at U.1.a.5.7. about 600 yds away. The magnitude of the mining operations were not made known to our Corps prior to zero hour, and consequently the sudden firing of so many large mines, had momentarily a bad effect on steam. During the central attack the Bn had on its right flank the 13 Cheshire Regt. "C" Co on the right, and "B" Co on the left, the 6 of Royal North Lancashire Regt. "D" Co on the right and "B" Co on the left entered NUTMEG TRENCH between N36.d.58.30 and N36.d.30.73 at zero + 35 seconds, no serious opposition encountered, at zero + 7 mins NUTMEG RESERVE between N36.d.95.42 and N36.d.89. was captured. "D" Co and "A" Co moved forward in succession immediately behind "C" & "B" Co. Battalion H.Q. were in rear of "A" Co. "D" Co then went forward and captured the line BELL FARM to O.31.c.6.7, which objective was taken at zero +20	

WAR DIARY
or
INTELLIGENCE SUMMARY.

(Erase heading not required.)

Army Form C. 2118.

Place	Date	Hour	Summary of Events and Information	Remarks and references to Appendices
	June 1917			
	7	3.30 a.m.	Strong enemy dugouts which had withstood the bombardment were found in this line. They contained about sixty German, who would not come out until bombs had been hurled amongst them. Enemy was killed in this fighting. Few newcomers were made prisoner. From the beginning of the assault, owing to the darkness at the time of launching the attack, and the almost unrecognizable state of the ground, direction was lost by most units in the percent, and only in the advance upwards became very mixed. After the BELL FARM line had been taken A & B Coy went forward with the Co. on their left and joined in the assault on OCCUR TRENCH at 3.40 & 3.50 minutes. Here some twelve more prisoners were secured. Luckily at this stage there was a general movement to the left flank, as our men entered L'ENFER WOOD, which was on the front of the 96th Division who were near on the battalions left, as the 8th Loyal North Lancashire Regt were now consolidating on these objectives in rear.	

Place	Date	Hour	Summary of Events and Information
MESSINES RIDGE	June 7 1917	5.5 a.m.	C & D Coy now in accordance with plans moved forward to assist the 1st Wellington Regt in the capture of their ultimate objective. OCTOBER SUPPORT, which was taken at zero + 4.C.T. However, prisoners were taken here, and in dug-outs in the vicinity. The Brigade had now reached its furthest objective. Consolidation of each objective was taken in hand immediately on its capture. Battalion Hd. Quarters had now moved forward again, and was finally established at HELL FARM. O.31.E. S.S. The assault being finished the Battalion Companies disposed themselves as soon as possible, and a start was made to carry out the tasks of consolidation which had been assigned to them. D & C were employed [?] was dug along a [?] from O.32.C.3.4 & O.31.C.P.G. and a C.T. started from this line to HELL FARM. Throughout the whole of the attack the men had shown the greatest eagerness to press forward, and there is little doubt that some of them ran into our own barrage. Seven [?]

WAR DIARY
or
INTELLIGENCE SUMMARY.
(Erase heading not required.)

Army Form C. 2118.

Instructions regarding War Diaries and Intelligence Summaries are contained in F. S. Regs., Part II. and the Staff Manual respectively. Title pages will be prepared in manuscript.

Place	Date	Hour	Summary of Events and Information	Remarks and references to Appendices
MESSINES RIDGE	June 7/17		was certainly lost at first, but the détriement disappeared later throughout the attack. The resistance of the enemy had been reduced very half hearted by the heavy shelling of the preceding days, and for the most part when reached showed little inclination to fight. Owing the advance the enemy did not systematically barrage any particular line, but there were fired indiscriminately over the whole battle front. Machine gun fire was also encountered at several points, some of it coming from indirect fire. There proved in rear. The carrying back done under 167 PARSONS dirt most valuable work, and throughout the day there was no shortage of water or essential R.E. Stores. Casualties. The battalion casualties were heavy, and in difficult to account for, a fair proportion must have been caused by our own barrage. The following officers were killed CAPT R.S. McDONALD & CAPT A.J.B. HOOSON	

T./134. Wt. W708—776. 500000. 4/15. Sir J. C. & S.

WAR DIARY
or
INTELLIGENCE SUMMARY.
(Erase heading not required.)

Army Form C. 2118.

Place	Date	Hour	Summary of Events and Information	Remarks and references to Appendices
MESSINES RIDGE	June 1917 7		2/LT F.W. BRAMPTON. Wounded:- CAPT. H. BIRCH-JONES, CAPT. L.N. MASON, 2/LTS A.V.P. ROWLANDS, R.S.R. MACKENZIE, E.W. LAZARUS, ST. DIXON, C.E.S. BRIMMELL. The casualties among N.C.Os and men were 24 killed, 8 missing, and 210 wounded.	Role substitution & nominal roll attached to this duplicate.
	8		The Battalion spent most of the day with its H.Q. at HELLFARM, and the companies in neighbouring trenches and shell holes. Strength marked this period the 7th Inf. Bde. was in support to the 75th Inf. Bde. who were holding the black line, and black dotted line about 100 yds in front.	appendices B, C, D and E.
		9.30 p.m.	The 7th Inf. Bde. relieved the 75 Inf. Bde. in the black line, and black dotted line. The Battalion took over from the 8 & 9 Lancashire Regt. and two companies of the 8th Royal Irish Lancashire Rgt. in OCTOBER SUPPORT and OCTOBER RESERVE Bn. Hd. Q. established in vicinity of MIDDLE FARM. Whilst him the battalion was in trench support. Enemy shelled intermittent during the day and night. Casualties for the day 2 O.R. killed, 6 wounded.	

T134. Wt. W708-776. 500000. 4/15. Sir J.C. & S.

WAR DIARY
or
INTELLIGENCE SUMMARY.
(Erase heading not required.)

Army Form C. 2118.

Place	Date	Hour	Summary of Events and Information	Remarks and references to Appendices
	June (1917)			
MESSINES RIDGE	9		The Battalion engaged in digging in the neighbourhood of MOOSE FARM, under R.E. supervision. A quiet day. 1 Lancashire & O.R. wounded.	K.M.
MIDDLE FARM	10		In the same position as on previous day. Enemy artillery very active during the evening about 7 p.m. and at intervals throughout the night.	
			Lt R. PIPER was killed by shell fire. Two O.R. also killed and two wounded.	K.M.
MIDDLE FARM	11	10 p.m.	In the evening the 7th Inf. Bde. was withdrawn from the line and moved back into Bivouacs at T.10.c.1.9. The 6th Yorkshire Regt. 11th Division took over the disposition of the battalion during the whole period the battalion had been in the battle area. the weather had been extremely hot.	
BIVOUACS T.10.C.1.9.	12		The day spent resting and refitting. The P.of and Divisional Commander made informal visits to congratulate the troops on their success during the recent battle.	K.A.C.
	13		The 7th Inf. Bde. moved back to relieve the 75 Inf. Bde. who were in	

Army Form C. 2118.

WAR DIARY
or
INTELLIGENCE SUMMARY.
(Erase heading not required.)

Instructions regarding War Diaries and Intelligence Summaries are contained in F. S. Regs., Part II. and the Staff Manual respectively. Title pages will be prepared in manuscript.

Place	Date	Hour	Summary of Events and Information	Remarks and references to Appendices
NEUVE EGLISE	June /17 13		Received orders close of NEUVE EGLISE at 7.9.C.3.3. The battalion took over from the 1st Cheshire Regt. A quiet day and nothing further to report.	
MESSINES RIDGE	14	10.0 p.m.	The bn afore named, the turn to the forward area and relieved the 13th Cheshire Regt, & the 7th & Inf. Bde. The 7th Inf. Bde became tripods in contact to the 75th Inf. Bde who were holding the Divisional front. Whilst in this position the battalion was distributed in old trenches about 500 yds S.W. of MESSINES. Bn Hd Qrs were in the old British front line at U.I.D.9.5. During the relief at about 12 midnight the enemy sent over a few shells, and confidentially hit a Co center, killing both hurts, and wounding the others. Thus O.R were wounded by this shell.	J.M.
"	15		Enemy shelled area occupied by the battalion at intervals during the day. Most of the shelling has been confined to 6 messines by street in collecting debris from the battlefield, and improving the trenches in which the men lived. Casualties 10 R. Women 30	J.M.

Army Form C.2118.

WAR DIARY
or
INTELLIGENCE SUMMARY.
(Erase heading not required.)

Instructions regarding War Diaries and Intelligence Summaries are contained in F.S. Regs., Part II. and the Staff Manual respectively. Title pages will be prepared in manuscript.

Place	Date	Hour	Summary of Events and Information	Remarks and references to Appendices
MESSINES RIDGE	June 1917 16		The day spent in the same manner as on the 15th. Enemy sent over odd shells during the day, and in the early morning bombarded the vicinity of Bn HQ with gas shells. 3 O.R. killed and 6 wounded	R.M
"	17		Nothing further to report on this day. Weather still continued to be very hot	
"	18		Thunderstorm in the afternoon about 4 o'clock. Weather appreciably cooler.	R.M.C
"	19		Nothing of particular moment occurred during these days.	
"	20		Intermittent shelling by enemy but most of it just missed	
"	21		the ground occupied by the Bn.	
"	22	15.20	The Battalion was relieved by the 31st Australian Regt. of the 3rd Australian Division. Relief was by 3.30 a.m. Bn were moved to RAVELSBERG Camp, and spent the remainder of the day resting.	
RAVELSBERG	26		Enemy occupied & put infraction etc. At 9.p. the Bn C. commenced a series of night marches back to a training	
D.C.18				

Army Form C. 2118.

WAR DIARY
or
INTELLIGENCE SUMMARY.
(Erase heading not required.)

Instructions regarding War Diaries and Intelligence Summaries are contained in F.S. Regs., Part II. and the Staff Manual respectively. Title pages will be prepared in manuscript.

Place	Date	Hour	Summary of Events and Information	Remarks and references to Appendices
	June 1917			
SWARTEN-BROUCK	24		area. The first halt was made at SWARTENBROUCK where the Bn. resumed march from horses.	
	25	9.30	March continued to TILLOTS close to ST VENANT, destination. In the night reached at about 2.30 a.m.	
ST VENANT	25		On again at 10.40 p.m. to WESTREHEM. A very wet night, raining practically all the way.	
WESTREHEM	26		At 10.20 p.m. resumed the march for COYECQUE, which	
			place it reached at 3 a.m.	
COYECQUE	27		Here the Bn. settled down for a short period of training. A very fine village, but billets not very good. A.D.C. a mile out of village, in fact in front in rear of. Men had two Companies had front rate billets.	
	28		Individual training commenced. Major Lieut Genl. Sir C.W. Jacob K.C.B. Commander of II Corps inspected the billets at COYECQUE at 10.45 a.m, and welcomed the 25th Div. back to his Corps.	

T.2134. Wt. W708-776. 500000. 4/15. Sir J.C. & S.

Army Form C. 2118.

WAR DIARY
or
INTELLIGENCE SUMMARY.
(Erase heading not required.)

Instructions regarding War Diaries and Intelligence Summaries are contained in F. S. Regs., Part II. and the Staff Manual respectively. Title pages will be prepared in manuscript.

Place	Date	Hour	Summary of Events and Information	Remarks and references to Appendices
	June 1917			
COYECQUE	29		Company training continued. Special attention devoted	Apprx 30%
"	30		to training for open warfare.	F.
				List of award given for real carried out in fruits and for recuperation in France &
			E.A. Chaffee Major Comdg 2nd Wisc Regt	
			S.O. 6.17	

T2134. Wt. W708—776. 50C000. 4/15. Sir J. C. & S.

Casualties During Month of June.

Date June	Officers K	Officers W	Officers M.	Total Officers	Other Ranks K	Other Ranks W	Other Ranks M.	Total Other Ranks
Noon 1	-	-	-	-	-	1	-	1
2	-	-	-	-	1	14	1	16
3	-	-	-	-	-	1	-	1
5	-	-	-	-	-	4	-	4
7	3	7	-	10	27	212	-	239
8	-	1	-	1	2	7	-	9
9	1	2	-	3	-	5	-	5 * still at Duty
10	-	-	-	-	2	2	-	4
11	-	-	-	-	1	-	-	1
15	-	-	-	-	-	6	-	6
16	-	-	-	-	1	-	-	1
17	-	-	-	-	4	6	-	10
18	-	-	-	-	-	4	-	4
19	-	-	-	-	-	4	-	4
21	-	-	-	-	-	2	-	2

.... Major
COMMANDING 3rd WORCESTERSHIRE REGT.

Appendix A

SECRET 3RD BN THE WORCESTERSHIRE REGT. O.O. N° 142.

REFERENCE: PLOEGSTEERT. 28.S.W.¹/₁₀₀₀₀   1ˢᵗ June 1917.

1. "B" Co. will carry out an Enterprise on the front held by the 8ᵗʰ L.N. LANCS REGT. tomorrow night in conjunction with one carried out by that Bn.

2. The party will enter the enemy's trenches 40 yards on either side of NUTMEG AVENUE penetrating as far as NUTMEG RESERVE on the same frontage.

OBJECT. 3. The objects of the enterprise are to capture prisoners, and to find out how the enemy is holding his line.

ASSEMBLY FORMATION. 4. The attacking troops will assemble in the front line, between N.36.d.20.38. and N.36.d.12.44. by Zero – 30' and will form up in front of our parapet by Zero – 5' in three lines, as follows:–
First two lines, four platoon, under two Officers in line, each 16 strong, in two ranks, extended to two paces.
Third line, one L.G. section, 5 strong, on each flank, and one L.G. section, 7 strong, and 2 runners, under Lieut. A.I.B. Hudson, Cmdg "B" Co, in the centre.

ARTILLERY ACTION. 5. At Zero, a barrage will open on the enemy's front & support lines in accordance with the Artillery programme and the assaulting troops will follow up the barrage as closely as possible, about 8 yards distance between the lines.
At Zero + 2' the barrage will lift 100 yards beyond and parallel to the enemy front line.
At Zero + 4' it will lift on to NUTMEG RESERVE as a standing barrage, until Zero + and on penetrating barrage 100 yards East of Nutmeg Reserve.

(2)

(3)

TIME
Everyone in possession of a watch will synchronise it with that of the Signal Officer at Zero – 30'.

PRISONERS
Prisoners taken will be kept under close arrest at Bde Headquarters at T.6.c.8.

Handcuffs will be utilized as far as they will go, in securing prisoners; 1 pair will be sufficient for 2 men.

IDENTIFICATION
No papers or distinguishing marks will be carried by anyone. Every man will carry a small card bearing his name and number which will be handed to the Co. S.M. on re-entering our trenches.

RETURN
Pl. Cmdrs will not return from our front line until all their Pl. are in.

On re-entering our trenches, troops will pass through them as quickly as possible but the pace and actual route followed will depend on the enemy's retaliation.

MEDICAL ARRANGEMENTS
8 Stretcher Bearers will await the return of the party in our front line and will convey any casualties to S.A.M.'s but first

BOMBS
Bombs will be distributed at the foot of NORTHUMBERLAND AVENUE at Zero – 60'.

APPENDIX F

List of awards given for raid carried out on June 2nd and for major operations on June 7th.

Regt^l No.	Rank and Name	Date	Remarks
	MILITARY CROSS		
	Lieut. A.J.B. HUDSON	2 June '17	Since Killed in Action 7-6-17
	" C. GREENHILL	2 "	
	DISTINGUISHED CONDUCT MEDAL		
13422	Sergt THOMPSON S.	2 June '17	
	MILITARY MEDAL		
40169	L/Cpl FISHER W.	2 June '17	
6350	Sergt CASSON J.	— " —	
40187	Pte GOWER J.	— " —	
	MILITARY CROSS		
	Captain A. BIRCH-JONES	7 June '17	
	" I.N. MASON	— " —	
	2/Lieut. F.M.H. JONES	— " —	Attached 8th Border Regt. since wounded and died of wds.
	DISTINGUISHED CONDUCT MEDAL		
12361	Sergt FORREST W.J.	7 June '17	
23141	Corpl CURRALL W.	— " —	
10863	Pte JASPER C.	— " —	
	MILITARY MEDAL		
23224	L/Cpl HAGGER W.	7 June '17	
17054	Corpl COOK D.	— " —	
8293	Sergt JOHNSON W.	— " —	
28759	Pte SPEED J.	— " —	
13268	Corpl BATE A.	— " —	
19905	L/Cpl CORNFIELD H.	— " —	
8425	Pte MORAN F.	— " —	Attached 7th Inf. Bde

Army Form C. 2118.

½

3rd Worcestershire Regt

Vol 35

WAR DIARY
or
INTELLIGENCE SUMMARY.
(Erase heading not required.)

Instructions regarding War Diaries and Intelligence Summaries are contained in F. S. Regs., Part II. and the Staff Manual respectively. Title pages will be prepared in manuscript.

Place	Date	Hour	Summary of Events and Information	Remarks and references to Appendices
	July 1917			
GODEWAERSVELDE	1		Bn. Training & resting at GODEWAERSVELDE	
	to 5			
	6		Bn. moved by motor buses to STEENBECQUE & transport by road	
	7		Were entrained by motor buses to neighbourhood of POPERINGHE & thence by march route to HALIFAX Camp	
YPRES	8		Bn moved up to YPRES in the evening. Enemy shelled at HALIFAX CAMP & the ESPLANADE from 2" & howrs Regt, 8" Div.	
HALIFAX Camp	9		Bn relieved 2" R Berks Regt 8" Div in trenches in the HOOGE sector between J.18.c.5.5. & Bovr. 3 Blo. (J.24.d.2.8. N.w.) also J.19.c.1.9. & 1.5.5. Bn lies in the sup. & 10" shells Regt in sup.	
	10		Bn in trenches. broken to battery. Offensive patrols. Enemy very quiet & apparently withdrawn behind the ridge. Artillery fire on both sides increased. (Tunnelling Coy.)	
			tried saying the length the Bn relieved 1st trenches in front of present front Line Day of 193 O.R. found killed.	J.83
YPRES	11		Bn relieved by 6th L.N. Lancs Regt. & proceeded to billets in YPRES, one before in railway embankment & Moat Villas, one & three others Delta	

Army Form C. 2118.

WAR DIARY
— or —
INTELLIGENCE SUMMARY.
(Erase heading not required.)

Instructions regarding War Diaries and Intelligence Summaries are contained in F. S. Regs., Part II. and the Staff Manual respectively. Title pages will be prepared in manuscript.

Place	Date	Hour	Summary of Events and Information	Remarks and references to Appendices
YPRES	Aug 1917 18th (?)		Bn in the support trenches. No enemy activity in the front areas.	
	19th		One Co relieved one Co 8" L.N. Lanc in trenches. Some shells not of great intensity experienced by day at intervals.	
	19th		Relief by 8" L.N. Lanc Regt completed as usual.	
	20.		2/Lt A.R. PING & 2 other ranks who formed part of a patrol which entered the enemy trenches near the HOOGE crater, with the intention of examining dug outs filled with rubbish were attacked by the enemy & failed to return.	
	21.			
	22.(?)		P.Cte Legrand not yet returned which ended the enemy patrol in trenches without casualty by ourselves.	
	23.			
	28.		Bn relieved by 2" Southern Lancs Regt & 8" Dur. & Norwich & HALIFAX Coy	
HOOGE STRT	24		Bn moved at 9.33 pm to bivouac at B26 d 4.3.	
	25(?)		Bn moved to bivouac refitting training	
	30(?)			

P.R. Whalley
LIEUT. COL.
COMMANDING 3rd WORCESTERSHIRE REGT.

APPENDIX "A"

Casualties for July 1917

Date	Officers			Total Officers	Other ranks			Total Other ranks	Remarks
	K	W	M		K	W	M		
9 July 17					-	1	-	1	2/Lieut A R Ping
11 " "					1	1	-	2	
13 " "					-	4	-	4	
16 " "					-	9	-	9	
17 " "					-	6	-	6	Includes 12 O.R
18 " "					-	2	-	2	wounded slightly,
21 " "			1.	1.	-	11	2	13	still at duty.
22 " "					1	1	-	2	
23 " "					-	4	-	4	
Totals	-	-	1.	1.	2	39	2	43	

30 July 1917.

.... LIEUT. COL.
COMMANDING 3rd WORCESTERSHIRE REGT.

3rd Bn. THE WORCESTERSHIRE REGT. O.O. 152

Map Ref. BELGIUM. 28. NE
BELGIUM 28. NW.

Appx: B

JULY 30th 1917

1. The Bn will parade in FIGHTING ORDER at 10-45.pm. tonight, with head of the column on the main road just beyond the ORDERLY ROOM, in column of route in the following order:—

   "A"   "B"   "C"   "D".

2. Distances of 200 yds will be maintained between Cos throughout the march.

3. On arrival at the position of ASSEMBLY H.22.C. the Bn will form up in QUARTER COLUMN.

   Men on falling out will remain in the immediate vicinity of their Platoons.

4. On moving forward to the HALFWAY HOUSE AREA all N.C.Os and men will be equipped as follows: (a) Rifle Secs:
   Pick or Shovel. (1 pick to 4 shovels)
   (b) Bombing Secs:
   6 Mills Bombs in bucket or Waistcoat Carriers.
   (c) Rifle Grenade Secs:
   4 Mills and 4 Hales Rifle Grenades in bucket. Co: dumps of same will be made on arrival at the objective.
   (d) Lewis Gun Secs:
   16 Magazines in 4 bucket carriers.
   In addition, all N.C.Os and men will carry two Sandbags and 1 Aeroplane Flare; wirecutters and wire breakers as issued, will be divided between sections, the loop wire cutters being carried by riflemen.

5. CAPS will be collected by C.Q.M Sgts on arrival at the assembly area.

   Officers Valises will be stacked at the present transport lines by 6pm tonight.

6. Each Co. will detail a carrying party of 10 men under a N.C.O. These with four pack ponies will report to Q.M. Stores in the assembly area at...

notified later.

7. All ranks of "B" Team will remain in present bivouacs until after breakfast tomorrow when they will march to H.28.c.

8. From the assembly area, the Bn will advance at ZERO + 4 hrs in column of route with distances of 50 yds between Pls.

On reaching the canal bank, H.Q. details and EVEN Pls will take the EGG road and No 7 TRACK and ODD Pls C TRACK and No 6 TRACK.

On arrival at HALFWAY HOUSE, Coys will proceed at once to DUGOUTS which have been shewn to Co: Commanders.

9. The Bn will advance to the RED LINE in two lines of Pls in column at 30 yds interval and 200 yds distance. "C" and "D" Cos in front, the right platoon of each line resting on the right boundary line of the Division and the left platoon being in touch with the 10th CHESHIRE REGT.

"C" and "D" Cos will at once send out patrols to get in touch with troops on their flanks and in front.

Immediately the SUPPORT LINE, which is to be taken over, is reached, each Co: will send forward an OFFICER'S PATROL to get in touch with the advanced Bn and Co: H.Q. of 8th of the 25th INF: BDE.

P. Haymann Lieut
Adjt. 3rd Bn The Worc: Regt

Issued at 1 pm.

Army Form C. 2118.

WAR DIARY
or
INTELLIGENCE SUMMARY.
(Erase heading not required.)

3rd Monmouthshire Regt.

Vol 36

Place	Date	Hour	Summary of Events and Information	Remarks and references to Appendices
	19.7		Bn. ordered from reinforcement RESERVE BATTN to Divisional BELGIAN château area	Ref. Map
		3:00 A.M	Battle of Pilckem commenced. (See A.F.C.B.)	28
		3:00 A.M	Bn. left the HAI FARM HOUSE dumps (I.17.c.0.3) for field dressing station to move forward to the Ridge near the RED line, to be in the 8th Divisional reserve [illegible]
			move forward [illegible] objective and to protect the flank of the 8th Div [illegible]
			At 4.15 H.Q. front line reached trenches NE of Wieltje on 78 Rd.
			A + B moved to BELLEWAARDE RIDGE in [illegible] 2nd Bn. Middlesex Regt position
			to relieve 12 R Bde of 4th Division Ridge. This [illegible]
			[illegible]
		10:30 A.M	The situation being [illegible] [illegible] were sent up to 25th [illegible]
			Bn relieved by Oxford Regt. & moved to MALDEN camp	J.34

Army Form C. 2118.

WAR DIARY
or
INTELLIGENCE SUMMARY.
(Erase heading not required.)

Instructions regarding War Diaries and Intelligence Summaries are contained in F. S. Regs., Part II. and the Staff Manual respectively. Title pages will be prepared in manuscript.

Place	Date	Hour	Summary of Events and Information	Remarks and references to Appendices
	1917			
	5 Aug		[illegible handwritten entries]	

WAR DIARY
or
INTELLIGENCE SUMMARY

Army Form C. 2118.

Place	Date	Hour	Summary of Events and Information	Remarks and references to Appendices
	19/7		Bn. received orders to join 1/15th London Regt. (which had left two days previously) reports them in marching order. Bn. proceeded to railway siding near POPERINGHE entraining at 2½ hours and proceeding to CHAPELLE in billets arriving approximately 6 p.m. and into billets. Capt. HD WILLIS OC A & HQ, 2nd Lt O. Gillette as acting Adjt. Bn. OM & Lt. W. H. HUGH (1/15 London Regt.) as acting Orderly Room Sgt. Maj. 2 R&F, 12 R.F.A. (1/15 London Regt.) Canteen for a/c of OR, 12 R.F.A. 41 horses, 3 mules & 20 men to the Tr. Supply, 40 O.R. to the 1/5th London Regt. B.L.	
	12		Bn. at SS by route march from RAILWAY dugouts by road made over CHEESECRENTINGHE & CLLIERS to C.S. STEENVOORDE.	
	13		Bn. in billets near STEENVOORDE. Training continued on the day.	

WAR DIARY
or
INTELLIGENCE SUMMARY.
(Erase heading not required.)

Army Form C. 2118.

Instructions regarding War Diaries and Intelligence Summaries are contained in F.S. Regs., Part II and the Staff Manual respectively. Title pages will be prepared in manuscript.

Place	Date	Hour	Summary of Events and Information	Remarks and references to Appendices
			Bn. arrived near STEENVOORDE, training.	
			Bn. moved to YPRES by lorry. Thence by march to HIGHWAY HOUSE, relieving 11th Royal Scots, 23rd Div. to be in the reserve to be holding the line. Relieved J19687 & J8C62.	

Brevelle .... LIEUT. COL.,
COMMANDING 3rd WORCESTERSHIRE REGT.

Appx: A

Casualties during month of August 1917

Date	Officers K	Officers W	Officers Total	Other Ranks K	Other Ranks W	Other Ranks M	Other Ranks Total	Remarks
31.7.17		1	1	1	9	.	10	Officer Casualties Lieut C Dodd
1.8.17				.	3	.	3	
2.8.17		1	1	14	63	-	77	Lieut A W Vinel slightly, at duty. 11 O.R. wdd slightly at duty
3.8.17				1	11	.	12	
4.8.17		1	1	2	5	.	7	Lieut L.P. Brettell
5.8.17				4	12	.	16	
10.8.17	1	2	3	10	41	.	51	Lieut C Greenhill "Killed" Lieut T Randle "Died of wounds 11/8/17." Lieut H S Kemp
11.8.17	1	1	2	12	49	2	63	Captain J M Evans C F "Killed" Capt H S Willis RAMC "Died of wounds 12.8.17"
12.8.17				.	1	.	1	
20.8.17				2	2	.	4	Other wounded slightly at duty
24.8.17				.	1	.	1	Accidentally
28.8.17				.	1	.	1	- do -
Total	2	6	8	46	198	2	246	

31st August 1917

.... LIEUT. COL.
COMMANDING 3rd WORCESTERSHIRE REGT.

Army Form C. 2118.

3rd Worcestershire Regt

Vol 37

WAR DIARY
or
INTELLIGENCE SUMMARY.
(Erase heading not required.)

Place	Date	Hour	Summary of Events and Information	Remarks and references to Appendices
	3rd August to 5 Sept		Bn in Bde Reserve in vicinity of HALFWAY HOUSE. Heavy shelling at intervals. Showers magnificent form. Relieved at 9pm on 5th by 11th Cheshire Regt 75th Inf Bde. On relief Bn marched back to camp near DICKEBUSCH	
	6th " 7		Resting & refitting at DICKEBUSCH.	
	8th		Started march to First Army area. First halting place WYTSCHAETE hrs near ABEELE.	
	9th		Bn in billets near ABEELE.	
	10th 11th		Bn marched to camp near CAESTRE. Bn marched to billets at THIENNES, near STEENBECQUE. (Bn now in I Corps).	
	12th		Bn marched to do BURBURE, where it was to stay for a period of training.	

Army Form C. 2118.

WAR DIARY
or
INTELLIGENCE SUMMARY.
(Erase heading not required.)

Instructions regarding War Diaries and Intelligence Summaries are contained in F. S. Regs., Part II. and the Staff Manual respectively. Title pages will be prepared in manuscript.

Place	Date	Hour	Summary of Events and Information	Remarks and references to Appendices
	13th to 30th		Bn in training at BURBURE. Very good training area. Many & varied recreations arranged eg boxing, sports, football concerts etc. Weather extremely fine throughout. Divisional Fête held on 26th - a great success.	

P R Whalley
LIEUT. COL.
COMMANDING 3rd WORCESTERSHIRE REGT.

Casualties during September 1917.

Date	Officers			Other Ranks		Total Other Ranks	Remarks
	K	W.	TOTAL	K	W		
Sep 1				1	2	3	
2		Nil			1	1	
3				1	6	7	
4				-	5	5	
5				1	3	4	
				3	17	20	

30th Sept. 1917

.... LIEUT. COL
COMMANDING 3rd WORCESTERSHIRE REGT.

WAR DIARY
or
INTELLIGENCE SUMMARY.

(Erase heading not required.)

October 1917

3 Worcester Regt

Place	Date	Hour	Summary of Events and Information	Remarks references to Appendices
BURBURE	Oct 1 to 3		The Bn still in billets at BURBURE, where it continued training.	
BETHUNE	4		Bn marched to BETHUNE where it billeted for the night. The whole Bn was accommodated in the tobacco factory.	
GIVENCHY FESTUBERT SECTOR	5	6.30 p.m.	The Bn proceeded to the trenches at the hour, and relieved the 1/7 Middlesex Regt of the 6th Inf. Bde. The relief was made after dark. The front held extended from the Northern end of WARWICK SOUTH ISLAND A 3 C 95 65 on the right to the junction of SHETLAND ROAD, and kent line at S 22 c 38 15 on the left. The frontage being about 2100 yds. The 1/10 Cheshire Regt held the line on our right, and the Portuguese on our left. The relief was carried through without incident, and completed about 11.15 pm. The sector held by the Bn contains no period of actual importance. It is all low lying, and is dominated by the GIVENCHY RIDGE on the right flank. The trench system is temple, and consists of two means lines of trenches. Small isolated posts are held in front of our front front line, which is not continuous in all places.	

Army Form C.

WAR DIARY
or
INTELLIGENCE SUMMARY.
(Erase heading not required.)

October 1917

Place	Date	Hour	Summary of Events and Information	Remarks references to Appendices
GIVENCHY PESTUBERT SECTOR	5		The old British front line now approximately 1000 yds in rear of the line now held, and in the former Bn Hd Qrs are situated. The shelter for the most part are very old, but owing to these having been built entirely of this kind of late, are in very fair condition. At the times of taking over, however, owing to there being in every observance of water scouting in.	F.W.
	6		much of the ground in water. A wet morning. Very quiet day	F.W.
	7		Nothing to report.	F.W.
	8 9 10		Uneventful days. Nothing to report	F.W.
	11		The Bn. was relieved in the line by the 8th Loyal North Lancashire Regt. and became battalion in Bde. Support at WINDY CORNER. Hd Quarters and two companies went in billets here, no company garrisoned the front KEEPS on GIVENCHY RIDGE, and the other company was accommodated in the OLD BRITISH FRONT LINE.	F.W.
WINDY CORNER	12-17		In support at WINDY CORNER during this period	F.W.

WAR DIARY or INTELLIGENCE SUMMARY.

(Erase heading not required.)

Oct 1917

Place	Date	Hour	Summary of Events and Information	Remarks & references to Appendices
GIVENCHY FESTUBERT SECTOR	17-23		The Bn relieved the 8th Royal North Lancashire Regt, and during its tour of six days had the 6th Cheshire Regt on its right, and the Portuguese on its left. A considerable amount of rain fell the first two days but after that the weather cleared. Some trench mortar activity at times. Bn had two men killed and six wounded by T.M's.	J.H.C.
GORRE CHATEAU	23-29		On relief by the 8th Royal North Lancashire Regt. the Bn moved into Bde reserve at GORRE CHATEAU. Here the Bn found six guard days. A few working parties to the forward area were found these days.	J.H.C.
GIVENCHY FESTUBERT SECTOR	29 30 31		Again took over from the 8th Royal North Lancashire Regt. and had the same troops on either flank. Nothing to report beyond the fact that Lt. Hope, 2nd in Co. 4th S. Staffordshire Regt. was struck down this tour for instruction, has just arrived from England.	J.H.C.

P.R.Walle.
LIEUT. COL.
COMMANDING 3rd WORCESTERSHIRE REGT.

CASUALTIES DURING OCTOBER

Date	Officers			Total	Other Ranks			Total	Remarks
	K	W	M		K	W	M		
Oct 6	-	-	-	-	-	1⁰	-	1	⁰Slightly at duty
" 22	-	-	-	-	2	1	-	3	
								4	

7th Inf Bde

Herewith War Diary for month
of October 1917

_____ LIEUT. COL.
COMMANDING 3rd WORCESTERSHIRE REGT.

To 7th Bde
in trenches